# BOOK REVIEWS

### An Unforgettable Journey

"I feel like this book takes one on a physical, emotional, and spiritual journey. Its heartfelt love and warm hugs you like a blanket in the winter cold, so you never want to let it go. It's truth tugs at your heart and slaps you in the face like a good reality check. The deep and rich illustrations reflect the universal themes of life. Cherish each moment definitely comforts, challenges, and inspires every generation to take care of what really matters most."

-Blackgirlsmatter2020

### This book is amazing!

"The book is excellent and so touching. It reaches the heart and really makes you give your love ones their flowers while their alive. I'm so happy I purchased this book and you will not regret ordering it either."

-Tammy

### A MUST READ!

"If you value relationships with others, you will definitely enjoy this book as it reminds you to enjoy life no matter what season you're in. CHERISH EACH MOMENT make you reflect on your life and encourages you to keep your family as a priority."

-Jennifer

### Words to reflect and inspire every day!

Ms. Jackson puts her family experiences and hopes eloquently into these beautiful poems. "Moments of Wisdoms" is one of my favorites.

-Nico Jimz

### This book will bless you!

This is a powerful, faith-filled exhortation to love those around us with the time we have. Combination of prose, poetry, and song, alternating between heartfelt reflection and powerful exhortation. Your faith will be uplifted and you will be inspired to bless others. A wonderful addition to your library.

-Rachel Alberg

### Open Book

This book is filled with more than just words and proses. This book is filled with authentically raw experiences of people of God. The beautiful, the complex, the painful. Each person who reads this book can see parts of themselves or others they know within these pages.

-The Countess

**Inspirational**

A well, written book! I liked how it embraced different topics of life. I read some poems and stories to my daughter and she had a few favorites of her own. A must read, you will not regret it!

-Zany

Mary's book inspires everyone to learn and to celebrate their lives with gratitude towards God.

-A Loretta

# CHERISH
# EACH
# MOMENT

*POETRY, SPOKEN WORD, INSPIRATIONS,*
*& REFLECTIONS*

# MARY E. JACKSON

**Cherish Each Moment**
*Poetry, Spoken Word,*
*Inspirations, & Reflections*
*Mary E. Jackson*

*iUniverse Publishing*

**Cherish Each Moment**
**Poetry, Spoken Word, Inspirations, and Reflections**

*iUniverse books may be ordered through booksellers or by contacting:*

*iUniverse*
*1663 Liberty Drive*
*Bloomington, IN 47403*
*www.iuniverse.com*
*844-349-9409*

*Because of the dynamic nature of the Internet, any web addresses or links contained in this book may have changed since publication and may no longer be valid. The views expressed in this work are solely those of the author and do not necessarily reflect the views of the publisher, and the publisher hereby disclaims any responsibility for them.*

*Any people depicted in stock imagery provided by Getty Images are models, and such images are being used for illustrative purposes only. Certain stock imagery © Getty Images.*

*ESV*
*Unless otherwise indicated, all scripture quotations are from The Holy Bible, English Standard Version® (ESV®). Copyright ©2001 by Crossway Bibles, a division of Good News Publishers. Used by permission. All rights reserved.*

*KJV*
*Scripture quotations from the Holy Bible, King James Version (Authorized Version). First published in 1611. Quoted from the KJV Classic Reference Bible.*

*NIV*
*Scripture quotations marked NIV are taken from the Holy Bible, New International Version®. NIV®. Copyright © 1973, 1978, 1984 by International Bible Society. Used by permission of Zondervan. All rights reserved. [Biblica]*

*The Message (MSG)*
*All Scripture quotations are taken from THE MESSAGE, copyright © 1993, 2002, 2018 by Eugene H. Peterson. Used by permission of NavPress. All rights reserved. Represented by Tyndale House Publishers, Inc.*

*Unless otherwise indicated, all Scripture quotations are taken from THE MESSAGE, copyright © 1993, 2002, 2018 by Eugene H. Peterson. Used by permission of NavPress. All rights reserved. Represented by Tyndale House Publishers, Inc.*

*Scripture quotations marked MSG are taken from THE MESSAGE, copyright © 1993, 2002, 2018 by Eugene H. Peterson. Used by permission of NavPress. All rights reserved. Represented by Tyndale House Publishers, Inc.*

*Amplified Bible (AMP)*
*Copyright © 2015 by The Lockman Foundation, La Habra, CA 90631. All rights reserved. For Permission To Quote information visit http://www.lockman.org/*

*The "Amplified" trademark is registered in the United States Patent and Trademark Office by The Lockman Foundation. Use of this trademark requires the permission of The Lockman Foundation.*

*ISBN: 978-1-5320-8720-2 (sc)*
*ISBN: 978-1-5320-8719-6 (e)*

*Library of Congress Control Number: 2019917448*

*Print information available on the last page.*

*iUniverse rev. date: 11/09/2020*

## *Dedication*

In loving memory of my beautiful mother, Annette Jackson (February 3, 1943-October 22, 2008).

Cherish Every Moment was inspired by my mother's words before her passing. Her wisdom has inspired me to write a song in honor of her memory.

# *Foreword*

I have known Mary Jackson for over 30 plus years. I have had the privilege of working with her in ministry for over 20 years. She has always had a love for writing. When she said she wanted to be a bestselling author, I strongly encouraged her to go after her dream and write a book. I told her that if people don't laugh at your dream it simply means you're not dreaming big enough.

May this book be the first of many. Mary is very loving, caring, and passionate woman of God. She has a special way of encouraging and lifting people up through her words of poetry.

As you read her poems that are so beautifully written on the pages of this book, you may laugh, you might even cry but one thing I know for sure is that this book of poetry will bless your life, inspire you, and bring you hope.

May these poems make a powerful impact in the lives of all who read this book.

Rev. Latoya Moseley
CEO/Founder of Women of Destiny and The Kathleen Walker House
CO/Pastor of Bread of Life International Worship Center

## Preface

Your death can't steal the legacy of prayer, love, and praise you leave behind.
Your stamp on my heart will never depart.

You may have had your battle with cancer but nothing can steal your powerful witness
of faith, praise, and prayer. Even in the darkest of moments you refuse to complain, you
encouraged your loves one to cling to the one who has power over death.

You may have had a battle with cancer but you beat the odds, with God on your side
you're always a winner no matter the outcome.

So now you're dancing with Jesus you got the shackles off your feet.
No more pain, no more sickness holding you back.

# *Introduction*

Each day I'm alive, I strive to see my time here on earth as reason to cherish, celebrate, appreciate, and love. Two scripture verses, (Ecclesiastes 3:1, 8 NKJV), perfectly illustrate the reason for me creating this book. *The Bible says, "To everything there is a season, and a time to every purpose under heaven...a time to love."*

Many people today are struggling to survive their moments of life when, I believe our Heavenly Father desires us to truly experience love and life. The typical picture of a person surviving life is usually a picture of someone barely hanging on by a thread. I think we need to learn to daily renew our faith each moment in the Holy Word of God. There is nothing sharper or more powerful than the Word, which is essential to meeting our daily needs.

This book was birthed from my mother, Annette Jackson's final words that still resonate with me today, "Cherish Each Moment." This book offers readers a time to evaluate and observe each moment in their lives as a gift from God. It's time to cherish, celebrate, and commemorate each and every moment of our lives.

In everyday moments, good or bad, happy or sad, tough or easy moments, God is always present for those who take the time to earnestly seek Him and allow Him to be the Lord over their lives. It is my prayer that as you read these powerful words of love, hope, faith, and wisdom that you will embrace a more intimate relationship with the only One who can truly help and bless you to "Cherish Each Moment."

# Contents

**Dedication** ......................................................................................... vii

**Foreword** ............................................................................................. ix

**Preface** ................................................................................................ xi

**Introduction** ...................................................................................... xiii

I. Teachable Moments ............................................................................. 1

    **Battle Ready** ................................................................................... 4

    **Pastor Appreciation Acrostic Poem** ............................................... 5

    **ADJUSTING TO GOD?** ................................................................. 7

    **Harmony** ....................................................................................... 9

    **Yes, You Can, Do Anything!** ........................................................ 10

    **LIFE'S CHOICES** ....................................................................... 12

    **STEP BACK, DEVIL** .................................................................. 13

    **Light Acrostic Poem** ................................................................... 15

II. Moments of Wisdom ........................................................................ 17

    **Peace** ........................................................................................... 20

    **Life-Light** .................................................................................... 21

    **Reflections** .................................................................................. 25

    **PRAY** ........................................................................................... 26

    **Dream Gateway** .......................................................................... 27

    **Apparently You Don't Understand** ............................................... 28

    **Can You Hear Me?** ...................................................................... 29

    **Sharing the Wonders of the King** ................................................ 31

    **SHOOTING STAR** ...................................................................... 32

    **Identity** ........................................................................................ 35

    **My Song** ...................................................................................... 36

III. Moments of Faith .......................................................................... 37

    **Mother of Mine** .......................................................................... 40

    **Promises** ..................................................................................... 41

    **A Graduation Message and Prayer for You** ................................. 42

    **Crucified Flesh or Living Flesh** .................................................. 43

IV. Defining Moments .......................................................................... 51

    **New Birth** .................................................................................... 55

    **Goodbye Sin** ............................................................................... 56

    **LIFE OR DEATH** ....................................................................... 57

For the Love of God ............................................................................... 59

Sincere Neighbor ................................................................................... 61

FROM SCARLET WOMAN TO SCARLET CORD OF DELIVERANCE 71


V. Moments of Love, Mercy, and Grace ................................................. 75

Destiny Acrostic Poem .......................................................................... 78

THE ONLY NAME ................................................................................ 80

Love ...................................................................................................... 81

Love Acrostic Poem ............................................................................... 82

EVERYTHING ..................................................................................... 83

I DON'T KNOW WHY ......................................................................... 85

BEST OF ME ......................................................................................... 86

Audacity of Forgiveness ........................................................................ 87

You Are ................................................................................................. 94


VI. Remembering You/Memory of You Moments .................................. 95

Cherish Each Moment Song .................................................................. 98

Each Day .............................................................................................. 100

INSTANT REPLAY ..............................................................................101

Missing You ......................................................................................... 103

Never Easy ........................................................................................... 104

Homeward Bound ................................................................................ 105

Farewell ............................................................................................... 106


Conclusion............................................................................................ 107

Author Bio............................................................................................ 109

Acknowledgments.................................................................................111

Synopsis................................................................................................112

# I. Teachable Moments

**"Study to shew thyself approved unto God, a workman that needeth not be ashamed, rightly dividing the word of truth." 2 Timothy 2:15 KJV**

The word of God states, "It's more blessed to give than receive" (Acts 20:35 NIV). As an educator, I desire to teach out of love, compassion, mercy, passion, and the overflow from heaven. In order to do so, I must strive to be a giver not a taker, and an individual who is ready for life's many lessons.

For one to think they know-it-all is beyond absurd. Each day you are blessed with new learning opportunities, if you have a teachable spirit. It's our responsibility as leaders and teachers to be teachable so we can grow in knowledge instead of deepening our ignorance.

God desires his sons and daughters to spiritually grow to become what He initially created us to be. Being like Christ is more than professing to be a Christian, speaking spiritual words, wearing a cross, carrying a big Bible around, or sporting religious gear. It's about denying of self, taking up your cross, and following our Lord and Savior Jesus Christ. Remember you can't have the resurrection without the crucifixion. You can't have the good and reject the bad that comes your way. In life we will experience moments of happiness, joy, suffering, and pain; however, God will guide us through each moment.

Do you have a desire to truly contribute to the world? Do you have an inner longing to become all God intended you to become? If yes, you need to give yourself completely to God. As a result, the seed you plant in His rich soil will sprout and reproduce beyond your wildest imaginations.

This personal inquiry means, you need to ask yourself the question, do I have the spirit of discipline to pay the price for spiritual growth and maturity. If not, ask HIM and you will acquire it. God is ultimately the best teacher to grow you in the faith. But, it will take much effort on your part. It's not about being perfect. God can take our inadequacies and turn them around for our good.

Anyone that humbly takes heed to instructions is destined to be wiser than before. Lessons come in many shapes and forms. God expects his children to grow. If you're not growing it means you're stagnant and shrinking. My prayer is that God will give you a passion to grow and mature in him. We are blessed to know that God looks pasts our mistakes and reminds us of our worth daily.

I'm committed to becoming the best teacher and learner I can possibly be. I'm tired of having to repeat some of the same lessons over and over again because of my own hard-headedness, disobedience, and trying to do things my own way. Ask yourself the question; am I committed to learning and growing? "Give instruction to a wise wo/man, and s/he will still be wiser; teach a just wo/man, and s/he will increase in learning" (Proverbs 9:9 NKJV).

It is my prayer that you will whole-heartedly embrace your own teachable moments as they appear in whatever shape or form. I'm praying this over your life,*"... Asking that you may be filled with knowledge of his will in all spiritual wisdom and understanding, so as to walk in a manner worthy of the Lord, fully pleasing to him, bearing fruit in every good work and increasing in the knowledge of God"* (Colossians 1:9-10 ESV).

# BATTLE READY

Are you truly ready for battle?
Or
Are you about to be defeated?
Are you daily being beat down?
If so, are you willing to do what it takes to overcome your adversary, the devil?
Do you want to be armed dangerously and prepared for spiritual battle?
Do you know the weapons for spiritual warfare?
*Faith, prayer, the Word, worship & praise*
Do you have the Code of Conduct?
*The Holy Bible*

Stand straight or fall flat on your face.
Bend your knees to Me or be trampled to
the ground in total disgrace.
Cry out to Me so you will be spared the pain,
the agony of disobedience,
and the consequences of sin.
The decision as to whether you will be on the victor's side
or the losing side is up to you.

Let Jesus set you free!

**Inspiration**: This poem was created when I shared a message titled "The Battle Is Not Yours, It's The Lord's," for Teens Who Love Christ Youth Ministry. I enjoy encouraging young people in their spiritual journey with the Lord to stand firm in their faith.

# Pastor Appreciation Acrostic Poem

"**PASTORS** and teachers are to prepare God's people for works of service, so that the body of Christ may be fully built up" (Ephesians 4:11-12 ESV).

**AGAPE A**cknowledging **G**od's **A**nointed **P**astors with **E**ncouragement "Love the Lord with all thy heart, and with all they soul, and with all thy strength, and with all thy mind" (Luke 10:27 NIV).

"**SPEAK** Lord for thy servant heareth" (1 Samuel 3:10 KJV).

"**TRUST** in the Lord with all thine heart: and lean not unto thine own understanding. In all your ways acknowledge Him, and He shall direct your paths" (Proverbs 3:5-6 KJV).

**ORDAINED** by God. "Ye have not chosen me, but I have chosen you, and **ORDAINED** you, that you should go and bring forth fruit, and that your fruit shall remain: that whatsoever ye shall ask of the Father in my name, He may give it to you" (John 15:16 KJV).

**RESPECT** those in authority over you. "**RESPECT** the Holy One of Israel" (Isaiah 17:7 KJV).

**AMBASSADOR** proclaim the gospel of Jesus Christ. "We are **AMBASSADORS** for Christ…" (2 Corinthians 5:20 KJV).

**PRAYER** invades the impossible, shaking and shattering the world of darkness. **PRAYER** warriors, "pray without ceasing" (1 Thessalonians 5:17 KJV). "Fervent **PRAYERS** of the righteous woman availeth much" (James 5:17 KJV).

**PRAISE** continually. "Let every living thing, breathing creature **PRAISE**" (Psalm 150:6 Message). "I will bless the Lord at all times and his **PRAISE** shall continually be in my mouth" (Psalm 34:1 KJV).

**ROYAL PRIESTHOOD**, be set apart. "But ye are a chosen generation, a **ROYAL PRIESTHOOD,** holy nation, a peculiar people; that ye should shew forth the praises of him who hath called you out of darkness into his marvelous light".
(1 Peter 2:9 KJV).

"**EDIFY** one another in the body of Christ" (1 Thessalonians 5:11 KJV).

**CHOSEN VESSEL**. "Many are called, but few are **CHOSEN**"
(Matthew 22:14 KJV).

**INTEGRITY** is the benchmark of a great leader and it preaches a powerful sermon. "The just wo/man walketh in his/her **INTEGRITY**: his/her children are blessed" (Proverbs 20:7 KJV).

**ANNOINTED VESSEL**. "Touch not mine **ANOINTED**, and do my prophets no harm" (2 Chronicles 16:22 KJV).

**TRUTH** will set the captives free. "Study to show thyself approved unto God, a workman that needeth not to be ashamed, rightly dividing the word of **TRUTH**" (2 Timothy 2:15 KJV).

"**INSTRUMENTS FOR NOBEL PURPOSES**, made holy, useful to the Master and prepared to do good work" (2 Timothy 2:21 NIV).

"**OVERCOMER** by the blood of the Lamb and the world of our testimony" (Revelation 12:11 KJV).

"**NO GOOD THING WILL HE WITHHOLD** for those who walk uprightly" (Psalm 84:11 KJV).

Inspiration: I wrote this poem for Pastor Appreciation, as a tribute to my Pastors' Rudolph and Latoya Moseley. They are the senior and co-pastor of Bread of Life International Worship Center. I truly believe that appreciation should be on going not just designated for a special month, time, or season. This poem is meant to offer them both words of encouragement and words to live by as they live out the call of God on their lives and actively serve Him.

# ADJUSTING TO GOD?

Are you submitting your life to God?
Are you fighting the good fight of faith? (1 Timothy 6:12)
You say,
you want God to bless you,

but you're still warming the pews.
You're still talking, not walking
You're still looking but not actively participating
You're still doing your own thing, not obeying His Will.

Will you trust Him or experience a rough ride of indifference?
Will you adjust and bend to His Will or will you go astray
and BE LEFT BEHIND?

He wants to bring you into a
NEW SEASON,
but you settle for the mediocre
limiting yourself to what is comfortable to you.

Your lackadaisical attitude has thrust you
into a lukewarm, murky
existence that will quickly advance you to a

slippery
slope
downward

if you don't press the brakes fast.

The vision He has for you is greater
than you can ever imagine.

By reading and applying His Word,
praying unceasingly and fervently on a daily basis,
and walking in obedience
I will illuminate the narrow path ahead for you.

Although,
your future seems unsure

know that the plans He has for you
are not to harm you but to give you
a hope and a future.

Don't let anything
keep you from the numerous blessings.

Fear will paralyze you
and keep you bound in sin.
Stop being afraid!
Step out in faith
and experience a deeper depth.

IT'S A NEW SEASON.
THE BEST IS YET TO COME!

# HARMONY

There are some things in life that you can't live without.
You may say that money, food, water, clothes, and friends rank at the top 10.
I say the absence of rules breed chaos and confusion.
*Rules* are what help to keep us safe.

Pause for a minute, think about the word RULES for a quick 60 seconds.
Where can you expect *rules* to follow you?
Are they in the air or on the sea?
Do you feel they are all unnecessary?

What do you suspect will happen if *rules* all disappeared?
Everybody in the world would be hassle free.

Do you imagine a peaceful existence or something entirely different?
Personally, I like the idea of having *rules*, it helps to maintain order and eliminate disorder.

What *rules* are all about can be spelled out in 7 little letters R-E-S-P-E-C-T.
If you show respect in what you say and do, you will not have to worry about breaking the *rules*.

**Inspiration**: In 2003, I wrote this poem to accompany the Discipline Plan for my students.

# YES, YOU CAN, DO ANYTHING!

**YES, YOU CAN**
do much more than you settle for each day.

**YES, YOU CAN**
be more than some people think or say.

**YES, YOU CAN**
blame everyone else for where you are,
right now,
instead of taking full responsibility for your own actions.

**YES, YOU CAN**
make all the excuses you want
**but**
your circumstances will never change
unless the change starts within you.

If you dare
to do something different then,
and only then,
can you expect different results and better outcomes.

Unless you do something different you will not gain something new.

My students see your potential;
**YES, YOU CAN**
be anything you want with great effort, hard work, endurance, stamina, and faith.

**YES, YOU CAN**
achieve anything if you only believe and put your faith into action.

Life's not easy
**but**
don't get played by the devil,
don't get played by the world
or play yourself,
by accepting less than your personal worth.

Reach your potential,
don't forfeit your dreams.

Aim for the stars
and
you will never fall short in this journey called life.

Don't end up working two jobs
instead of one good one you can have with a college degree.

There's a saying, "the only difference between a job
and career is education." *Stay in school!*

Don't withhold your best!
Give your all!
Don't give up!

**Inspiration:** In 2008, I wrote this poem as an End of the School Year Poem for my students. The words, "Yes, You Can" from President Barack Obama's campaign inspired me to write this poem for my "kids" as I call all of my students that I have been privileged to educate throughout my teaching career. These powerful words I pray will impact my "kids" lives in such a way as to spur them on to be difference-makers, history makers, and world changers. I want all children to dare to believe that they can make a difference wherever they are; they can be change agents that are solution oriented, and service oriented, meaning they offer solutions to problems and render a helping hand as needed.

# LIFE'S CHOICES

Life's choices are too important to mess up.
What you decide today will affect your tomorrow.

If you choose to go the broad way it will lead to your destruction
If you choose go down the narrow road it will lead to your salvation.

You only have one life to live so make wise decisions and choices.
**Choose life!**

Don't try to fit in with the crowd because they will lead you to the
**POINT OF NO RETURN**.

Don't be a chicken, be an eagle, so you can soar high above the obstacles
that will present themselves in your life. **Chickens fry and eagles fly**.

Don't fall into the traps and snares of peer pressure, drugs, alcohol,
cigarettes, gangs, crime, and any other deadly controlling habits.

Your dreams can come true if you don't go astray
and you stay focused on the tasks ahead of you.

Stay in the race, don't get off course!

You are somebody special!!!

You can be whatever you want to be, when **YOU** believe anything is possible.

Don't let anything stand in your way.
Always work hard and do your best.

**Inspiration**: In the Spring of 2002, at the time when I only taught sixth graders I wrote this for my students.

# STEP BACK, DEVIL

**Step back, Devil** you think you can slay me with your lying lips and your shady tricks, using the Word of God will make you trip.

I call on my Abba and He says, *darling speak my Word* and you'll go hollering, evaporating into thin air like the sinking sand foundation in which your words are fashioned.

The One I serve unlike you is rock solid, built to endure.

**Step back, Devil** I have news for you, your days are numbered and few.

You think you are living large and in charge.

However, Jesus Christ far surpasses any false façade you hide behind.

The image you portray as powerful conqueror is the total opposite of your true colors: impotent, adversary, defeated foe.

You as angel of light, conqueror, sheep, merciful, charming, honest, powerful, friend, life-preserver, provider how totally absurd.

Really you are the prince of darkness, defeated, wolf, merciless, ugly, a conniving liar, weak enemy, murderer, thief, and full of deceit.

You come as an angel of light when in all actuality you are a fallen angel turned demon by your twisted thinking.

**Step back Devil,** you will find no footstool here, for the trap you set will in the end be the one to trip you up for an eternity in hell.

You need to be reminded that God is always near and you should fear.

For in the presence of the Holy Ghost demons have to flee.

**Step back, Devil** your reign is a figment of your imagination, the consequence of your giving birth to the darkness of sin.

You foolishly think you'll get the best of mankind but all you'll get is hell's kick and be burnt crisped.

God's way is victorious, He's magnificent to your indifference.

**Step back, Devil** you're living in a fantasy world you designed from lie after lie;
and one day you'll wake up to the point of no return where hell will be a reward for your
rejection of God as your Sovereign King, too bad you were a mutinous foe.

Once and for all the light of God's love will expose the truth that you are one big joke.

**Step back!**

# LIGHT ACROSTIC POEM

**LET** your **LIGHT** illuminate the darkness in the world. "Let your **LIGHT** shine before men, that they may see your good works, and glorify your father in heaven."

Matthew 5:16 KJV

**IMITATE** God in your conversations and mannerisms, "Therefore be **IMITATORS** of God [copy Him and follow His example], as well-loved children [imitate their father]."

Ephesians 5:1 AMP

**GODLINESS** is emulating God. "…Pursue righteousness (right siding with God and true goodness), godliness (which is the loving fear of god and being Christ-like), faith, love steadfastness (patience), and gentleness of heart."

1 Timothy 6:11 AMP

A **HEART** after God is daily dying to self and to individual will. "Blessed are the pure in **HEART**: for they shall see God."

Matthew 5:8 KJV

**TRANSFORMED** to fit the standard of God's Holy Word. Living out God's Word in our everyday lives. "Don't become so well-adjusted to your culture that you fit into it and in turn compromise your faith. Instead, fix your attention on God. You'll be changed from the inside out. Readily recognize what he wants from you, God brings the best out of you, develops well-formed maturity in you."

Romans 12:2 MSG

# II. Moments of Wisdom

**"But the wisdom that is from above is first pure, then peaceable, gentle, and easy to be entreated, full of mercy and good fruits, without partiality, and without hypocrisy." James 3:17**

**M**oments of wisdom are like nuggets of knowledge that are invaluable.
Do you feel like your spiritual journey is one in which you constantly battle the feeling of being lost? Maybe you feel like your Alice in your own wonderland and you have fallen down the rabbit's hole.

Are you in search of wisdom? Does wisdom seem to be elusive to you? Does it appear like you are on a personal wilderness journey that only you share? You are in search of a way out of your puzzled life and you're searching for the knowledge you lack.

Life experiences and adversity are the bedrocks to the development of wisdom. The Bible Says, "The fear of the LORD is the beginning of wisdom: and the knowledge of the holy is understanding." (Proverbs 9:10 KJV) If you fear the Lord you are on the threshold of wisdom. I believe the Lord is saying to you, my son or daughter, if you are open to gleaning from Me you will learn much more than you already know. You can't expect the wisdom; I give to come without a price for its active pursuit. Wisdom initially starts from reverently fearing Him and then it extends once His will replaces our will and we obediently listen and obey His instructions regardless of the variety of ways it comes.

# PEACE

When things go wrong, as they always do
remember a friend who always remains true.

He longs to be your guiding light.
He will never lead you astray,
all you have to do is just trust and obey.
He said, "Come unto me all you that our heavy laden and I will give you rest."
I know it's hard but fright not my child
you have nothing to fear because I have all your cares in the palms of my hands.

Don't be afraid because I will make the crooked straight,
mend the broken-hearted, heal the sick, save, and set free from all bondage and sin,
despair, hopelessness, and depression, if only you let me in.

Only remember it's me my child who you are to cast all your cares upon.
No matter what your problems and circumstances seem to say,
surrender them all and they will soon fade away.

The Almighty God is waiting there with arms open wide
If you just won't delay.
Respond today with yes, okay.

RESPONSE:

Lord, I'm willing to stay come what may.
In your arms I know I will find comfort, peace, love,
and rest for my weary and burdensome soul.

I truly believe you will give me more of your power, love, and strength for today and bright
hope for tomorrow, to lift me especially through the most trying of times.

Heavenly Father, thank you for being ever faithful
and true and so wonderful to one so undeserving but ever grateful for you.

I know you love me and I love you too
With your help I will pray and serve you every day,
No matter what may come my way.

Love, your faithful servant.

# LIFE-LIGHT

Are you the Life-Light for the world to see
or are you dim from deep within?

Christ came so that His greatest creation,
could experience abundant life, not a piece of it.

Don't you know that God wants to be the main course not just an appetizer or dessert.

Why do you choose to settle for some,
when you're not even willing to accept
what your Creator has in store?

You're missing out
on this ultimate gift of life!

This gift can't be bought or sold.
Many have tried to work for it,
bargain for it, plead for it
but they eventually realize
the uselessness of their endeavors.

Why can't you see the light must be lit within
and JC is the only true Light.

You can't come by way of
Mohammad, Confucius, Buddha, Joseph Smith,
or other man-made gods and prophets.

Reject your infatuation with cheap god-imitations.
If you allow Him, God will lead you,
down the road to redemption and eternal life.

Many people would rather
choose a lie than the genuine article,
they're addicted to denial and illusion,
making it a common practice of perpetuating sin.

These individuals hate God-Light
and won't even come near it.

They lust for what they don't have
and are willing to do whatever to get it.
They know not to ask God for it
because it's not in His perfect plan for their lives.

You spoiled children, wanting your own way.
Quit dibbling and dabbling in sin and playing the field.

There is "plausible deniability"
since God knows the truth
not the lily white façade
you try to hide behind.

He sees the inner man, the inner woman
not your false claim to innocence.
Purify your inner life.
Get real serious about the King,
get down on your knees
for it's the only way
you'll really stand on your feet.

Honor, His gospel message,
don't defame it.
You'll end up enemies with God
if you don't change your ways.

The simple thing would be to choose
this free gift at no expense, no cost.
You and I are meant
to point out the way to the Life-Light,
like John the Baptist, the forerunner of the Gospel of Jesus Christ.

Be in the world not conformed to it
by taking on the characteristics of the culture
and allowing it to drag you down
to its level of immaturity.

Allow God to build His character deep within,
so you can learn how to go against the flow
of a godless culture.

Learn a sturdier faith that obeys no matter the cost.
Don't let the world affect your identity
or get you to compromise your purpose.

In the words of somebody else,
"Either we conform our desires to the truth
or we conform the truth to our desires," like Lucifer did.
Be like Christ.

Stop trying to fit into the world
and be separate from it,
let there be a distinction between the world and you, not conformation.

Look like Christ
and less like the latest superstar and fad.
Focus more on Him and less on things
that bear no real significance.

You will then find you will be in a better place:
spiritually, physically, mentally, and emotionally, not living in sin,
living to gratify your flesh
but instead walking in the spirit,
pleasing Him, loving Him,
trusting Him, serving Him,
believing Him, and obeying Him.

Don't work hard for sin your whole life,
squandering the potential you have for bigger and greater things,
for all you will gain is a pension of death in the end.

God's greatest gift for you is eternal life
The only way for true salvation is through His Son, Jesus Christ.
The One who wants to be the Lord over your life.
This Life-Light is the real thing.
When God gives something, He really brings it.
Our adversary, the devil
plots, plants, schemes,
to kill, to steal, or destroy.

But remember God has the final say.
Earth is not your home.
You can only experience
a little piece of heaven here on earth.
You can't expect to gain more.
If you look for more,
you will only fall into the trap Satan,
has in store.

Satan is only trying to distract you
with the world's poor offerings
to flatter your ego
and cater to your fleshly desires.
We are to be Christ representatives
of His presence here on earth.
We are to walk blamelessly and harmlessly
as children of God without fault,
in the midst of a crooked and perverse generation,
to shine as lights in the world.

Be a conduit of change not one that brings shame.
May you shine your light for the world to see your love displayed.

May you learn at your Master's feet,
His Holy Word, all error to discern
and by His Holy Spirit's light
will help you from Satan's snare to turn.
It's only God who can satisfy the longings of your heart.
Only He can fill the God-shaped void,
not treasure,
nor fortune,
not sex, drugs, alcohol,
a man, woman, or children
can satisfy in ways you cannot even measure.

Real evidence of a true believer
equals a transformed life.
What a waste of G-R-A-C-E
**G**od's **R**iches **A**vailable **A**t **C**hrist **E**xpense,
if what I profess does not add up to a dramatic change
in the way I live and conduct my life
I will never change my eternal destiny for the better.

# REFLECTIONS

Life don't mean a thing if you ain't got the King of Kings and the Lord of Lords.

What you have is one big façade wrapped up in a disguise as a gift, worth nothing but an eternal demise.

I'm not talking about a religious fling but a relationship with Jesus Christ, the King.

God doesn't want excuses.

He ask for a true surrender of body, soul, mind, and spirit, not lip service.

The gift that God gives is precious, genuine, abundant, satisfying everlasting, out of this world, and beyond your wildest imagination.

Why fill yourself with things that will last
and quench your thirst, or ease the hurt and pain?

God is calling you, don't delay when all you have to do is pray.

# PRAY

Father, forgive me, I know I've strayed and I need You to cleanse me from all sin.

I come in faith believing you died on the cross and rose again so I will not be lost.

I confess that I am sinner and need to be forgiven.

I want to make You the center of my life.

Come in today, I pray and stay always.

# DREAM GATEWAY

Dreams are a gateway to create possibilities of unlimited opportunities.
Without dreams you will be like a traveler on a journey going
nowhere, down a dead end street of aimless flight.

Dreams are a lighthouse to treasures that are disclosed
by the pursuit of aspirations and faith.

Grasp tight to dreams for if you don't life will be like a fleeting ship,
with no anchor to keep it rock steady and afloat.

Grasp tight to your dreams or your life will be like a caged bird
without wings to fly away and soar, with no hope for parole.

You will be bond by a desire to be free but forever stuck in defeat,
destined for a meaningless and aimless existence.

You will be imprisoned in a cage of your own making by indecision,
if you fail to dream and follow them.

**Inspiration**: This poem was inspired by Langston Hughes' poem "Dream Deferred." He is my favorite male poet.

# APPARENTLY YOU DON'T UNDERSTAND

You may think I'm crazy,
you may think I'm foolish.

I'm waiting on my Savior, Jesus Christ till He says it's ok.

I'll tell you, nothing,
shall stand in the way of the great blessing in store for my obedience.

Step back and get out of my way,
with your words that say I should go against my Lord and Savior.

I don't want a boy in mannish clothes.

I want a Godly, saved, sanctified, and filled with the Holy Ghost man.

You may be fooled by the trickery of the superficial mask but God is able to read the hearts
and minds of man
and see the real heart, not what is perpetrated by a flirt.

I don't want a playmate but a soul mate.

I'm praying, not preying.

I refused to be a casualty and squandered like a bag of dirty laundry.

God says,
Wait and baby,
I'd rather wait,
Then go rushing into a catastrophe and end up repeating a cycle of blasphemy.

**Inspiration**: This poem was inspired by a romantic breakup. These words are encouragement for anyone waiting on their Boaz, not Bozo, or Mr. Right or their Ms. Right not Ms. Wrong. Remember it's better to wait on God, than to wish you had waited for your lifelong mate or waited in any regards.

# CAN YOU HEAR ME?

It is a hard place between where I am, from where I want to be,
wrapped up in your arms throughout eternity.

The only thing keeping me strong and from running back to you
is the Chief Cornerstone, Jesus Christ.

If it was up to me, I'd be with you right now and never leave your side.
I don't know why the wait is so drawn out.

I sure hope God has not forgotten me.
I'm the one that's constantly, nagging you,
persistently wondering whether or not the answer is yeah or nay.

I want to be sure that it's you and not me directing this relationship,
from the start to the finish.

Please don't refuse my request for blessed peace, confirmation, and assurance.
I don't want to make a great mistake
and wake up to a living nightmare of separation and deprivation.
Let me keep holding on to You,
You are definitely a true friend.

**Can You hear me?**

Don't let me slide into depression, a mediocre existence of pain.
My heart longs to be free to love that special someone in my heart for now and always.
Lord, if he is not the one for me reveal it without a doubt
and help me to move on without looking back with misplaced emotions.

Father, forgive me,
for I desire to count on You and involve You in every decision I make.
Lord, I know, You know every detail down to how many hairs upon my head.

Help me to trust You to make everything alright and good, to correct what's wrong and
keep me going down the straight and narrow road.

My life will be meaningless without Your presence in my heart and in my life.
God, I am truly blessed to be your daughter.
I cling to the knowledge that my Heavenly Father will hear my prayers.

**Can you hear me?**

**Inspiration**: This poem was born as a result of my prayer to God for help and strength after a romantic relationship ended. My ultimate desire is to please my Heavenly Father and wait on the special mate He has for me. I do not want to foolishly or desperately rush into anything. I would rather wait on God's best for my life than wallow in regret.

**Can you hear me?**

# SHARING THE WONDERS OF THE KING

Are you sharing the wonders of the King
or are your lips sealed with silence that fear brings?

Are you proclaiming to the world:
the Good News of Jesus Christ's birth.

Join with the angels herald the King's appearance on earth.

Where will you find joy at Christmas time? Will it be
under a tree, filled with many gifts, Or

in a mad dash to the store in traffic galore?
Most definitely not!

Decide today the message you will spread about Christmas.
Will it be a message of hope, love, and redemption?
Or
will it be a scene of despair, hatred, and damnation?

The ONLY WAY you will experience a true time of jubilation
Is to know the CHRIST OF CHRISTMAS.

JESUS is the reason to celebrate the Christmas season.
If you leave Him out you will surely miss out.

Rejoice for the gift God's given in sending Jesus Christ, His Son.

**Inspiration**: The Christmas season inspired this poem. This poem was a prequel to an invitation to a Christmas Extravaganza event.

# SHOOTING STAR

Right now, you are uncertain of where the future will bring you.
But know that you have a special purpose,
a path that only you can follow.
With your faith in God, talents, gifts, insight,
and creative abilities you have so much to offer.

As you graduate
remember the unique qualities that you alone possess and bring to the world.
My nephew, JP, John, John Paul Jackson, Jr
you have been blessed with so many gifts and talents.

You are a basketball athlete like Michael Jordan and Kobe Bryant, a drummer like Vernel
Mincy AKA Dodder and Spanky a singer like Michael Jackson, Usher, and Tonae
a dancer like Michael Jackson, Chris Brown, and Robert Hoffman a comedian like Chris
Tucker and David Chappael a combination of so many talents and skills.

You are a divine instrument of God,
a shooting guard and small forward on the supreme basketball team.
As long as you stay connected to the true source of your power,
the Master Baller, Jesus Christ you will not lose your spiritual stamina,
endurance, and strength,
and your light will never go dim
it will brightly shine for all the world to see.

As you dribble down the court of life
you play for a place in heaven.
Remember the winner gains a reward that is priceless.
This is the game of your life.

You don't want to get fouled out of this game
for a foul out of this game means annihilation in Hell and an eternity in defeat.
Keep your focus on your role on this ultimate basketball team.
JESUS CHRIST, is the ONLY WAY, ONLY THE TRUTH, and ONLY THE LIGHT!
If you follow His lead as you journey down the court of life
from the start to the finish of the game
each maneuver you take will bring you closer and closer to your heavenly reward. He will
pierce the darkness of adversity, ignorance, depression, confusion, unbelief, pride, racism,
oppression, prejudice, mediocrity, compromise, doubt, anxiety, disobedience, rebellion,
complacency, fear, and suppression, and any other spirits, curses,

or forces that try to hinder His DIVINE WILL for you,
Follow your spiritual point guard, the Holy Spirit who wants to guide you to eternal victory.

As long as you follow his lead you will triumphantly soar to the Heavenly championship. JC is your point guard, the captain of your team trust Him for any and everything for the impossible is always possible for Him.

Whether you're on the basketball court, standing in front of a audience using your voice to sing or tell jokes, dancing, dedicate every basket shot, beat, lyric, dance move, wholeheartedly as unto the Lord.
Don't forfeit the game.
Keep your eyes on the prize.
The only way not to forfeit the game of your life is to stay connected through prayer and fasting regularly, reading the Word of God, walking in obedience, surrendering your will for God's will, praising and worshipping His name, fellowshipping with other believers regularly, and sharing the gospel with lost souls.

The basketball is like the sacred word of God.
You must hold onto at all cost not giving your opponent, the enemy the opportunity to capture it or take it away leaving you empty-handed and defenseless.
If you apply it to your life, you will reap its benefits in every area of your life.

Don't drop the ball, don't miss the shot of your life.
Don't let the buzzard beater ring to signify the end of the fourth quarter with you not ready to score the biggest win, the one for your soul's final destination.
"Choose ye this day to serve the Lord" and go the distance with Him.
In this game you need to guard against your opponent, the devil so you come out victoriously and undefeated.

The enemy is like the opposing team trying to steal the ball to score and win the game.
The Bible says, "the thief comes to steal, to kill, and to destroy."
Don't get played or seduced by the world and distracted into believing that it has anything worth having.

The Message Bible says in Romans 12:1-2, "Don't become so well-adjusted to your culture that you fit into it without even thinking. Instead, fix your attention on God. You'll be changed from the inside out. Readily recognize what he wants from you, and quickly respond to it. Unlike the culture around you, always dragging you down to its level of immaturity, God brings the best out of you, develops well-formed maturity in you."

Don't try to be a people pleaser, strive to please God and you will succeed with every endeavor. The favor of God is upon your life, be very careful to stay in sync with your athletic coach, musical director, dance choreographer, and vocal instructor.
Choreograph your steps with the most original chorographer, JC.

To your Lord and Savior Jesus Christ you are an MVP, the Most Valuable Player on his team.

Don't jeopardize your winning the game and gaining the victory for anyone or anything. The enemy wants to thwart God's plan for your life but fight in such a way as to win the prize. Go forth; be strong for the Lord your God is with you.

**Inspiration**: In 2008, I wrote this poem "Shooting Star" for my nephew, John Paul Jackson, Jr's graduation from Brandywine High School in Delaware. I often write poems using the talents and interest of the subject. Since my nephew loves basketball, drumming, singing, dancing, and comedy, I implemented these elements inside the poem I wrote for him and people he admires within his fields of interest.

# IDENTITY

Who am I?
I don't know the answer to that question.
I wonder why I was created.
Do I have a real purpose in life or am I a product of accidental birth,
without the hope of a future plan in sight?
I don't want to wander the earth aimlessly searching in all the wrong places,
faces, and things like boys, girls, a job, education, money
alcohol, drugs, sex, gangs, friends, babies, and more.

Will somebody help me find myself before I go crazy and do something
with eternal consequences? You wonder why I am the way I am, I'm so
confused, I don't know what to do, so I try many things to fill the void.
I feel stranded from finding my way in this journey called life.

I was told God is the only One who can make me whole and not leave a hole,
and give me a life beyond belief that will last throughout eternity.
What do I have to loose, I have tried everything else?
If He is the real thing, the genuine article, not counterfeit,
I will love and serve Him eternally.

One regret I have is that it took me so long to realize Jesus Christ is
the Only Way, The Truth, and The Light. I urge you not to fall into the
same traps I fell in. Embrace the Savior today before it's too late.

Only JC can put together the broken pieces of your heart,
mind, soul, body, spirit, and make them whole.
God leaves nothing broken and nothing missing.
Once you try Him there's no going back.

The only way is straight ahead,
an upward journey that leads to Heaven, join Me and soar now and forevermore.

**Inspiration**: I was inspired to write this poem by the ministry of Evangelist Fred Felton III of Impact Ministry. The words from his message to at a Youth Revival resonated so much with me that this poem was born. These words are for individuals that don't know that their identity can only be found in Christ or people who may forget and need to be reminded of this fact.

# MY SONG

The song, I sing is a celebration of who I am and want to be.
I am an African-American woman born proud and free.

You may like me, you may hate me but I know you didn't create me.
Who I am does not depend upon what you say or think about me today or tomorrow.
What you say to me face-to-face or behind my back doesn't mean a thing.
I stand tall, strong, and firm, I know I am not alone.

I'm a continuous note without pause,
Staying on tune following the vocal instructor, My Heavenly Father. The lyrics to the tune
I sing are angelic voices in a heavenly chorus, bridging a gateway to Heaven's Pearly Gates.
I sing in exuberant praise and jubilee for the many blessings that come from God down
to earth to me.

Every fiber of my being make me special and unique all wrapped up in one.
Each word, phrase, note, and tune I utter and sing is a glorious tribute to my Lord and
Savior, Jesus Christ.

Let the words, I sing, ring deep in the heart of all who hear me sing; bringing healing,
deliverance, peace, comfort, joy, happiness, salvation, and encouragement.

# III. MOMENTS OF FAITH

"But without faith it is impossible to please him:
for he that cometh to God must believe that he is,
and that he is a rewarder of them that diligently seek him." Hebrews 11:6 KJV

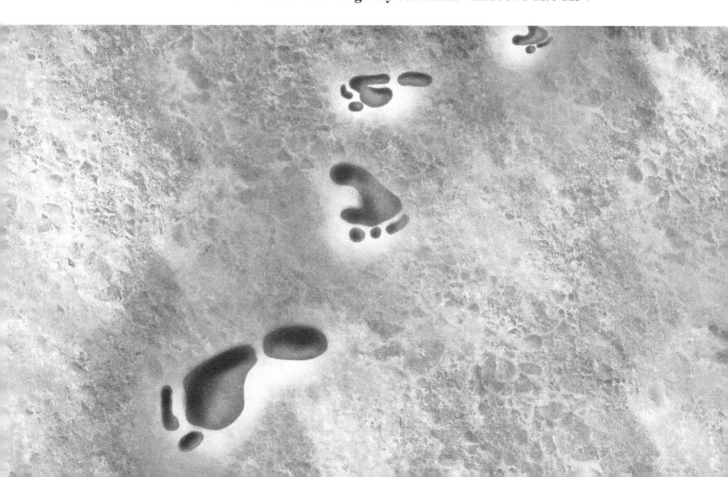

Y ou're walking down a darkened path, a road that begins to veer off towards the left, middle, and the right. Your feet are heavy with the weight of indecision. You are puzzled by the answer to the question of which way you are to go. A part of you wonders if the left may be the way to go. But inside you also think the road to the right looks pretty good in your sight. Nevertheless, the straight road ahead is beckoning you. Your mind and heart vaguely recalls hearing that you are to walk down the narrow road that leads to life for the broad ways lead to destruction.

The decision for the path you will take in your spiritual journey is completely up to you. You alone must decide if you will follow the Faith Road that is the narrow way or if you will go the way of the crowd down the Broadway Path.

Have you ever had to battle with fear in your life? What brought this emotion to the forefront? Was it because you wanted to venture out of your comfort zone, to try something new? Maybe you thought about participating in an extracurricular activity of some kind, switching jobs, careers, trying out a new business idea, investing money, getting involved in a new ministry opportunity- however, fear greeted you at every turn.

This fear made you question whether or not you should venture out into unknown territory. A part of you let this fear stop you from crossing over into a pathway of advancement. Nonetheless, some of you put distance between fear by rejecting its false implications and embracing endless possibilities with your faith in God.

The way of faith is not a road of ease but requires you to move past moments of darkness, doubt, denial, disaster, disobedience, and disappointments. The Faith Road is one that is full of constant challenges. If you let it, fear will corrode your confidence in God and prevent you from following His instructions. When doubt seeps in, it deadens you towards moving forward in victory.

If you let it fear will try to manipulate and dominate your life. It will prevent you from truly experiencing the abundant life your Heavenly Father desires to give you. The gift of faith is a powerful gift that God bestows on all His children. They must first be willing to believe in His promises that are written in His Holy Word and pursue Him at all cost.

God considers faith such an important part of the Christian-living experience that he makes it a requirement. Here's how significant faith is from the Bible, "But without faith it is impossible to please him: for he that cometh to God must believe that he is, and that he is a rewarder of them that diligently seek him." (Hebrews 11:6 KJV). This verse lets you know you can't please God unless you possess faith. God is saying whoever believes in Him and earnestly seeks after Him will be taken care of. It all balls down to whether or not we will take God at His Word and obey Him. If you truly fear God, you will obey Him. You must practice obedience to develop and cultivate it. It all boils down to what you think, you say, and what you do.

If you have minuscule faith you need to request that God gives you mustard seed faith, which has the power to move mountains out of your way. In (Matthew 17:20 KJV), Jesus gives some faith words to proclaim, *"…I say unto you, if ye have faith as a grain of mustard seed, ye shall say unto this mountain, remove hence to yonder place; and it shall remove; and nothing shall be impossible unto you."*

Jesus urges His disciples to speak to their mountains in faith. It's by your confession of faith that mountains will be removed. I dare say, that some of you have been saying the wrong things to your mountains, confessing defeat not victory, prolonging the mountains presence in your life because you're not properly applying the truths from this well-known passage.

Do you have mountains you desire God to move? Your mountains can be spiritual, mental, physical, psychological, financial, marital, academic, social, relational, job, business, or ministry related. Do you believe that the impossible will be made possible for the situations, problems, and challenges that you are currently facing now? Just remember, that God is a specialist of impossible dilemmas and struggles you face.

There will always be another level of faith that you need to conquer each day. You need to strive to conquer the faith for any given moment you face. Don't deny the Word of God and the promises of God. You are more than a conqueror.

Your feelings follow your faith. It's imperative that you make sure to confess with your mouth and believe in your heart the right theology and have a positive perspective. Life and death are in the power of the tongue so you need to make sure to declare, to rebuke, to confess, and to exercise your faith daily in little and big ways. For if you are not cautious you can destroy instead of create by your thoughts, words, or actions. You are to live the life of an overcomer and in order to do so you need to guard what comes out of your mouth.

Faith is what will carry us through your storms of life so "we must starve doubts and feed our faith." May God give us faith to trust Him for impossible things. May He remove your unbelieving heart and replace it with a faith believing one.

Moments of faith are a necessity in your faith walk. I pray you will experience deepen faith.

# MOTHER OF MINE

Mother of mine,
Mother of Thine,

You are a treasure among woman,
a vessel of tremendous purpose and worth,
special and precious in the sight of many.

You are loved beyond the measure of time and infinite stars.

Mother of intercession,
you are a prayer warrior
who shakes the foundation of hell
with your fervent prayers
rescuing the lost souls for the kingdom of heaven with your anointed
Holy Ghost power-packed prayers.

Mother of the Bible,
Mother of promise,
you have taken an unwavering stance on the solid Word of God.
The Holy Word is your compass
determining your spiritual longitude,
spiritual latitude, and your spiritual attitude
are aligned to the Only One that can lead you home.

# PROMISES

I know sometimes things are tough, but still keep pressing on.

No matter what may come your way, remember help will find the way.

I know it's hard but fret not my child, you have nothing to fear, this too will pass away.

I am by your side, I will never leave you child, just always obey.

I am El Shaddai, Jehovah God.

Don't cry, look to me and I'll be Your Guide to heaven.

# A GRADUATION MESSAGE AND PRAYER FOR YOU

May God guide every step you take.

You have come too far to turn around and give up.

You're in a spiritual battle you're sure to win if you follow Me,
I'll take you on a victorious journey that extends to Heaven's pearly gates.

I will protect you for sure if you pray and fast expectantly,
read my word, and obey my commandments.

Truly believe with Me anything is possible,

the only thing you need to remember is I'm your Sovereign Lord.

I have carried you this far you have no idea the direction I will take you,
if you lean upon the Rock of Salvation.

Always remember I will give you all you need, nothing can compare to Me.

I'll satisfy you totally and completely, not leave you with holes you'll strive to fill.

I love you unconditionally.
In all you do acknowledge Me and I'll direct your path.

Congratulations, on all the hard work you have done,
never leave Me out and you'll go far.

I'm proud of you and want to let you know,
every step of a righteous man or woman is ordered by Me.

Follow My footsteps all along the way and you'll see
me for sure beyond the pearly gates!

**Inspiration**: I wrote this poem when my sister graduated from college.

# CRUCIFIED FLESH OR LIVING FLESH

You,
follower of Jesus Christ,
and the body of Christ
your divine appointment is to seek and save the lost.

For far too long,
you have neglected evangelism and adequate discipleship
of new converts so they may grow and reach spiritual maturity.

STOP
just worshipping God and not truly serving Him.

You and I are to be women and men of action and greater works than Him.

Too many of us are too busy warming the seats of our various sanctuaries while souls are
perpetually dying.

It's past time for evangelism to rate higher
than acquiring the latest title or fad.

It's not enough for sinner's to be present to warm the chairs of our various church
establishments,
they need to be educated, and properly shown the way of righteousness.

What's the point of going to church,
if we're not willing to change
and apply the truths we hear
Going to church is not a penance for salvation

My mission as God the Father is to get you to be-all-you-can-be in ME.

It's my desire to go to the root of your problems
in order to set you free from every trace of them.

I love to use a divine DNA transfer to give my daughters' and sons' something they never had
to help them to be what they never were
but were born to be by My shed blood. (Isaiah 61:1-3 KJV)

I offer a way of escape.

At the moment of your salvation,
you received a divine DNA transfer.

New life, wholeness, & liberty
are a few blessings granted by My presence in your life.

Sin & the devil
are the enemies of your soul
but unfortunately in observing some of your lives
one would be fooled into believing they're your closest relatives not sworn enemies & foes.

Fortunately,
the Holy Spirit has not left us to our own devices, nevertheless,
it's up to us to listen and respond
in favor of the necessary changes to our lives.

Our pursuit of darkness over the light
leads us to acting cowardly instead of courageously like God instructs us to be.

Left up to your own futile thinking & defense,
"You'll call evil good and good evil." (1 Samuel 15:23 KJV)

Be led by the Holy Spirit not your flesh.

The word and prayer
are powerful weapons
against our biggest enemies
the world,
our flesh,
and our adversary, the devil.

For far too long,
we have sabotaged our destiny
by harboring the wrong things in our heart.

Often enough,
I informed you in My Word
that we were to engraft Your Holy Word into our hearts so we might not sin against You.

My Word is the best defense;
take it from someone who has personal experience using the Word to combat the forces
of darkness.

Your obedience to this means the difference between victory or defeat
good or evil
love or hate.

For once your heart & soul prosper so will the rest of you.

You're still striving to impress the world
that is busy watching and waiting
for authentic believers,
not hypocrites
who have become so deceived
into believing mediocrity is an acceptable everyday practice.

Compromise,
may not appear to be damaging in the moments it's embraced, however,
the consequence of this downward spiritual spiral is a subtle but deadly impact.

Once the spirit of compromise,
takes control,
it must be severed at the root
least it be resurrected for future harm and detrimental use.

You leave me displeased by your entitled indifference mentality, while I'm waiting for
your blinded view
to be illuminated by My truth that you need to allow to penetrate,
the perpetual mask you erect when I dare to correct your most unholy state.

Hi! It's me God.

Don't you know?

I'm supposed to be the undisputed boss of your life?

True kin of mine are connected
by a two-way intimate & personal relationship.

There should never be a moment
where it's one-sided communication
because we only call on God
to make demands
or when we have a problem we can't handle.

Kneeology is the only way the church and believers will stand strong on spiritual legs that
will not falter and get trampled down by oppositional foes.

PRAYER not unlimited time and access
on social media and other devices
has the POWER
to TRANSFORM us and our world for the better.

You and I must crucify our flesh daily
so we don't get disqualified
by our own ungodly cravings and indecent actions.

Crucified flesh = no attraction to the world & sin, thus giving the devil no foothold over me.

Though it's hard sometimes to witness God's plan and our role in that divine plan,
the two must be aligned for the desired effect of divine power.

STOP
allowing things that need to be put to death to be resurrected or kept alive so you can do
you instead of representing Jesus Christ.

Don't fail to remember the heavy price that was paid for our lives.

Don't play the fool and err exceedingly because your vow to God was just empty words
instead of a lifestyle of change & transformation.

You can't afford to squander your spiritual inheritance for
the world,
the flesh,
self,
or the enemy.

REMEMBER,
I am more concerned about your soul than your exterior.

Too much emphasis is placed on
eternal adjustments and makeovers
and not enough on true transformation.

At this point in my life,
Jesus Christ became our spiritual image consultant showing us how to look good from
the inside out.

I no longer strive to be good by the world's low standard but to be my best for His glory
and honor
based upon the Holy Standards found in the Book of Life.

If the Spirit is permitted to develop in you,
a clear image of Christ will most definitely be viewed by all who encounter you.

I was once spiritually dead,
till I met my Savior, Jesus Christ,
now I'm born again.

I have been given a new nature,
for I'm a new creation in Christ.

My past will not determine my future
but my obedience to God will.

Therefore,
we must stop evading real issues of sin
and deal with the reality
that we need God's help
to clean up our sinful lives so it's a thing of the past not what prevents us from going to heaven
and grants us instead a quick way to hell.

Our choices determine the outcome of our lives because we have the power over what we say and do, whether we believe You or reject Your Words
and choose to disobey.

Seek the One who blesses not the blessings themselves.

Seek to be a blessing rather than to be blessed.

Don't just stand by, stand up for the Lord, and lend a helping hand.

God, You have equipped me for every task ahead.

You tell us what we are to say at the right moment and teach us when we are to be quiet.

I know because you lovingly guide me every step of the way.

The godly should not be vanishing from the earth but should be advancing for the kingdom of God
to be influential in reaching past, present, and future generations with the Gospel of Jesus Christ.

Godly principles & godly ways should order our every step.
Too many of us have the gift;
but godly character is scarce among those called saints.

Are we self-seeking or God's servant?

Be faithful not faithless,
a servant not selfish,
forgiving not unforgiving
free not captive to sin
saved not lost

REMEMBER,
if our flesh is not crucified
it will be resurrected to life again.

If we give sin a place to roam free,
it will take a life of its own
that severs all ties with the King and Lover of your soul.

*For rebellion is the sin of witchcraft
and stubbornness is as iniquity and idolatry.* (1 Samuel 15:23 KJV)

Our spiritual hiatus,
our foolish interlude
needs to be a moment in our past.

We cease to exist to sin and live in right standing,
for we are called not to flesh moments but a lifestyle of holiness.

We are to be the picture of faith in action
a mirror reflection of Jesus Christ in all we do.

REMEMBER
the wrong attitudes will keep us out of our promise land.

REMEMBER
to regularly check if your flesh is crucified or if it's living in sin.
May your freedom
not breed the spirit of pride, excuses, or disobedience, because delayed obedience
will be a hindrance to your breakthrough for sure.

God's opinion is all that matters, our allegiance is to Him. We owe the only One who saved our soul from eternal flames, our allegiance.

You are a God of mercy,
a God of kindness,
and a God of Grace.

You don't give us what we deserve
but strive to give us what we need the most.

Thank you for your many blessings
that are new every morning & every day.

**Inspiration**: This poem is inspired by (Luke 19:10 KJV), **"The Son of Man has come to seek and save the lost."** The message from this verse is for the church to follow in the footsteps of Jesus and evangelize to the lost. It's time for believers to stop being comfortable with their soul salvation and where they are spiritually, to learn the Word, so they can hide it in their heart and actively apply it, to realize evangelism should be a high spiritual priority, and ask God for a zeal for the lost if they lack some.

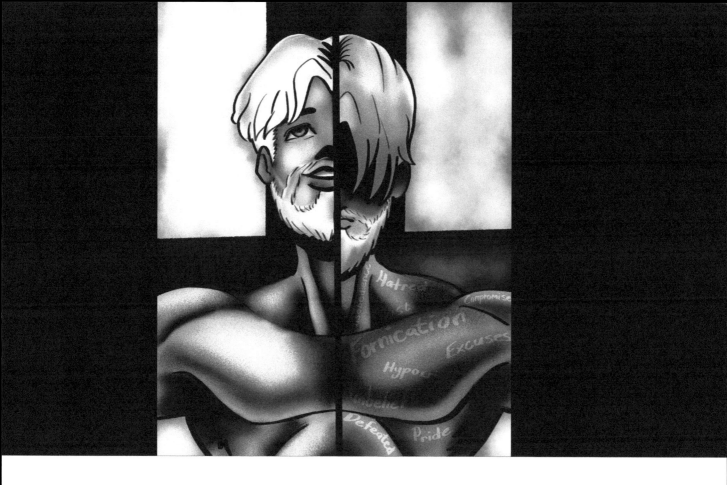

# IV. Defining Moments

**"Your destiny is determined by where you stand in the defining moment."**
**Be the Message Kerry & Chris Shook Pastors of Woodlands Church**

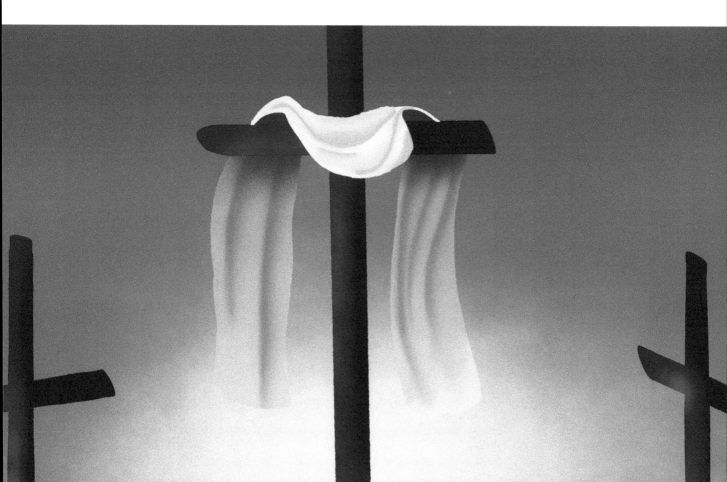

Have you ever had a moment that everything was hinged on? At that particular moment, you knew how you responded or reacted would affect the course of the history of your life for either good or bad. You wanted to make the right choice but the challenge was in what you did during the waiting period before your defining moment.

Authors of *Be the Message* Pastors' Kerry & Chris Shook say, "Your destiny is determined by where you stand in the defining moment." You have the power to positively gauge your destiny, if you determine now to always stand in faith with God.

Defining moments are moments that can make, shake, or break your faith. If you choose to allow them, they can make all the difference in your life. This type of moment has the power to cause you to go from victim to victor, lost to saved, weak to powerful, or a wimp to a champion.

If you choose to accept the defining moment opportunity it will alter your life for the better. However, if you decline this amazing step, your potential destiny will be overshadowed by a mock destiny of depravation.

"There is a defining moment in every person's life. Within that moment everything that person is shines brightest." Through this anonymous quote you witness how a defining moment reveals a person's true character. A defining moment has the ability to make you stronger, greater, or wiser. However, if what shines the brightest is a lack of faith the person is left weak and ignorant.

There comes a time when you must decide if you will take a stand for change or if you will let things remain the same. Those individuals who dare to take a stand for Christ will find out that they will experience a confrontation for living out the gospel message.

This direct challenge to your faith and your personal life message will be with the world's low standards and values.

You will always have moments of comfort-ability. If you are not careful this distraction can become a permanent fixture of your life by tempting you to set up residence there. For some reason, people expect life to be easy. As a result, this creates problems for them when the moment to take a stand approaches. Will you allow self-indulgence to take precedence over God's desire for getting you out of your comfort-zone? This distraction comes with a price, the death to a deeper intimate relationship with God. God's ultimate desire is for us to follow Him.

Always remember the rich young ruler, in (Luke 18:18-23 KJV), who came to Jesus wondering what he can do to be saved. Jesus told him there is one thing sell all you have. Well, this man is the perfect illustration of the problem of someone chosen to live or stay in their comfort zone. Apparently this man was religious and wealthy. The only thing Jesus said he lacked revolved around his reliance on his riches. The Bible says, he was saddened by this request to give away his wealth and he walked away. Here we witness a man living too comfortably on his security blankets of religion and wealth.

What has been your security blanket? Jesus Christ is to be our only security blanket. Jesus is still calling people to follow Him. The act of stepping out of your comfort zone enables you to learn who you truly are without any gimmicks. This step of faith opens windows of opportunity for God to work in your life. Here was a man who had a chance for a defining moment and he declined it on the basis of his comfort.

When you face your defining moment, will you deny Jesus Christ or will you stand for Him? My prayer for you is that when you face your defining moment; you will stand in victory not defeat.

# NEW BIRTH

Your spiritual new birth
was conceived on the day you received the Savior into your heart and life and welcomed a personal relationship with the Lord, Jesus Christ.

First, you admitted you were a sinner in need of the Savior, Jesus Christ.

Second, you believed in your heart that He died and rose again on Resurrection Day.

Third, by confessing your sins before your Creator and Savior you gained the best gift of all, eternal life.

Now, you have received the free gift of salvation, that can't be earned by man but was purchased by the blood of the Lamb.

At that moment of your spiritual conception,
you were commissioned to win lost souls for Him; to proclaim the Gospel of Jesus Christ to the nations not just with words but as a live-action messenger.

You are no longer identified by sin but forgiven of sin since you belong to Him.

Your heart and soul are set on fire.

You are doing your best to live for Him.

# GOODBYE SIN

Crucify the flesh or the old man/old woman will try to rise again.
Be not sin-serving but selfless in service.
For the dead are freed from sin's curse,
I'm raised to new life in Christ.
I reign in my mortal body
bring it under submission to thy spirit,
Most High God so I will not be disqualified by my actions once and for all.

I am an instrument of righteousness,
not an instrument of unrighteousness.

I yield to my God and bid sin goodbye
for it has no dominion and power over me.

I have been washed in the blood of the Ultimate sacrificial Lamb.
You're my propitiation who paid the atonement for my sins and suffered so I might live.

I say farewell to sin.

# LIFE OR DEATH

The decision you made to give your heart and life to the Lord Jesus Christ
is the most important decision you will ever make in your life.

MY CHILD, since you heeded my voice
and chose not to ignore my call for salvation
you are now entitled to all the benefits of one of my children.

YOUR INHERITANCE PACKAGE includes:
eternal life with Me throughout eternity,
death has no terror for you
because to be absent from the body is to be present with Me.

All I ASK of thee is that you
"Trust in me with all of your heart and
lean not to thine own understanding,
and in all your ways acknowledge Me and I will direct your path."

DON'T YOU KNOW
I will supply all of your needs according to my riches in glory
and I will never leave you nor forsake you."

REMEMBER the one to fear
is the one who has the power to put your soul in hell not man.
DAILY, PRAY, & LISTEN to my voice.

EVERYDAY READ MY HOLY WORD & OBEY my instructions.

Don't forsake the assembling of yourself with other believers since you find supernatural
strength in being surrounded by fellow brothers & sisters in Christ.

PRAYER gives you the supernatural power to LIVE AN OVERCOMER'S LIFE and not
succumb to anything.

When you READ MY WORD,
if you don't understand something all you need to do is ASK ME for clarification.

RIGHT NOW, MY CHILD
you are ready to meet death when it calls.
I AM ONLY A PRAYER AWAY. I LOVE YOU MORE THAN ANYBODY ELSE.

**Inspiration**: I was inspired to write this for one of my best friend's mom who I was privileged to lead to the Lord. By the time I led her in the Sinner's Prayer cancer had claimed her body and the doctors did not give her hope of life. This poem is a tribute to her, new converts, and believers.

# FOR THE LOVE OF GOD

*For the Love of God,*
when I was a little girl
I said the Sinner's Prayer
and received Jesus Christ
into my heart and life
and now He's here to stay.
FROM GIRLHOOD
TO WOMANHOOD
I take Him everywhere I go.

*For the Love of God,*
I remain steadfast in faith
growing in spiritual maturity
with each passing day I become more like Him.

*For the Love of God,*
I desire to glorify Him
in what I say, I do, and how I do it.

*For the Love of God,*
I pray and read the Holy Word daily
and attend church regularly
so I don't forsake the assembling of myself with other believers.

*For the Love of God,*
I don't walk in sin
for it shall have no dominion or power over me
I don't practice sin,
I daily practice the presence of God.

*For the Love of God,*
I dwell in the secret place of the Most High
for His presence makes the impossible possible for me.

*For the Love of God,*
I treat people the way God wants me to
so that means I love my enemies
even when hatred tries to take an ungodly place in my heart.

*For the Love of God,*
I claim my spiritual inheritance
as a daughter of the Most High God
SALVATION,
ETERNAL LIFE
PEACE,
& PROSPERITY to name just a few
because the promises of God
are by far too numerous to count.

*For the Love of God,*
I possess my Promise Land
no longer chosen to wander around
in the wilderness of disobedience, doubt, and denial.

*For the Love of God,*
I don't look for man to do what only God can do,
for I am complete in God not man.

*For the Love of God,*
I don't look at my problems
I hand my problems over to the Lord.
There's nothing too hard for Him.

*For the Love of God,*
I reflect His love
"Love starts with me."
I want to be like Him.

*For the Love of God,*
I'll be light and salt to the lost,
for I dare not remain silent
lest I have sinner's blood on my hands.

# SINCERE NEIGHBOR

You robbed me,

barely sparing my life's blood.

You nearly eradicated my presence with your strife,

your evil twisted belief that because

I'm black to your white

or another hue other than yours

I'm rich to your poor

I'm Eastside to your Southside

I speak another tongue other than yours

you think I must be less of a man, less of a woman,

less of a boy, or less of a girl

and better off left for dead.

You seized the opportunity to prey

on what appeared to be my weakness,

my inferiority, my vice, my wrongful place.

My differences overshadowed my humanity from your gaze.

You bared me naked before the world, you were without care.

To you my life was meaningless.

In your eyes I was a wasted entity

that you wanted to end without hesitation in your bias opinion.

On that life-changing day.

I was the darkness to your light.

I was deserving of a fatality,

your own version of morality.

I was deserving of your wrath

and your rejection was rightly founded

by the righteous indignation you sprouted.

You rejected my manhood, my womanhood,

my boyhood, my girlhood

on the basis of my lesser status to your higher status in your own eyes.

You pranced and danced in church

putting up a pious front that you were so holy and true

while all the time it was a superficial front,

a mask for prides conceit

of a falsified you

manifested by your sin.

Your uppity demeanor hid an ugly spirit within.

Beaten, almost left for dead,

my clothes had been stripped away.

Now left naked & destitute

the pain inflicted was deeper than the physical.

You left me there on the cold dirt

like I have reason to feel ashamed

for just barely breathing the air.

You were much too busy

pursuing worldly provisions to be a kind-hearted neighbor.

Your self-importance around God and other beings

has led you to this pitiful state,

you need to check at the door.

Why did you leave me on the side of the road and pass right on by?

Dejected and alone I waited for a kind soul to lend a hand.

But the first person that came by kept his distance and walked away.

Unceremoniously dismissed,

you shirked the responsibilities of a religious leader,

a priest, a Christian believer.

You left me by the way side and went about your regular day.

For your agenda was more important than someone in need of a friend,

a hand up not a putdown,

an opened door to a slammed one.

I'm suppose to look up to you, but you look down at me

in judgment because of my race, my color, and my other differences you say.

You resent me.

Your actions state I'm not worthy,

for I'm the wrong ethnicity.

I live in an inferior neighborhood.

I'm too different to be a friend

I must be a foe

not even worthy of your notice.

It's one thing to worship God in church

but quite another to practice what you learned

and bring it outside into your real-life experience

through daily obedience and looking for opportunities for service.

What a disservice?

For some of you it's easy and for the rest of us it's most difficult but some of us

quite frankly want to throw a wallet at the situation instead

of giving of ourselves to this predicament.

Worship must go beyond the walls of our church.

Don't you know you must be the church?

It's a listening to God's prompting to serve others

wherever and whenever above our own selfish will.

Yours and my worship & service

should not be confined to our own personal convenience.

Don't go through the emotions of church

but preach the most powerful sermon through your own personal life-example.

I cried out inside

*Lord, Lord, I needed a reassuring sign.*

Then the Levite came and I thought he would lend a hand

but all he did was avoid me by walking by to the other side of the road.

I failed to penetrate his constructed walls of indifference.

You were not a stranger but much too busy to be kind to your neighbor.

You have the time to be kind,

the ability to offer a lifeline

to someone knocked down by life's fatal blow.

Cold as ice, a mechanical puppet of self-righteousness & selfishness.

You see Me and others as interferences to your self-made plans,

and make excuses for your present pain,

just so you can run your own life even if it's straight into an early grave.

You turned a deaf ear to your heavenly Father's voice

or heard but chose to ignore His words.

You chose to ignore

a primary example of someone giving to the needy.

You checked out spiritually, physically, & emotionally, the day you decided

to flee a real relationship with Me and pursue a love affair with sin.

No wonder daily we witness a world more distraught by selfish acts

instead of giving of self away.

We seldom take the time for the needy to be kind, to be friendly

because we're perhaps too busy

accumulating & accessorizing

with more money, more cars,

more education, more pleasurable things.

With too much pressure we place on our agendas,

lost perspective overtakes our vision.

Your love for worldly things

has squeezed out your love for Me.

Worldly goods has captured you

leaving a hatred for what I love,

and a love for what I hate.

All you find important now has nothing to do with Me

but everything to do with appearing important to others and wanting your way.

All it does is set you up for hell,

nonetheless, those who do my will are set for all eternity in heaven.

Your leisure time weighs more

than spending time laboring and advocating for those in need.

Your standard of living by the holy perimeter has had a relapse,

a decrease because of your misplaced attention.

Watch your habits because they become your character.

You're selfish instead of helpful

Cold-hearted over kind-hearted

Your neighbor is not a stranger

but a brother or sister in need of love.

Your treatment of others

as anything other than God's son or daughter is blasphemous.

You sound so righteous, superior, and patronizing,

remove your robe of pomposity

& clothe yourself in humility.

Your religious babble is a bunch of hot air

getting ready to be popped by God

unless you deflate it yourself with a sincere changed heart.

You're a self-proclaimed know-it-all.

Yet you're illiterate & ignorant of matters of the heart

relating to Christ & a godly life.

You trade God for cheap imitations.

You'd rather serve your fake gods instead of the genuine One,

the One who created you.

You need a God habit & a word habit

not a religious compartmentalized or commercialized experience.

Give God access to your whole life

and he'll transform you from godless & loveless

to lovers of God & lovers of what He loves.\

Addicted to ease

although equipped by God for difficult things.

You were anointed by the Blood of the Lamb.

It's an "I can do all things through Christ who strengthens me endeavor,

not a one man, one woman, one boy, or one girl show.

Spiritual progress is offered to all but it must be pursued at all cost.

Discarded by 2 religious leaders, I mused on the event that left me here.

Next a Samaritan stopped by

I was sure I would receive rejection for the third time.

He shocked and pleasantly surprised me

when he was moved with compassion like the One they call Jesus Christ

and provided first aid & bandaged up my numerous wounds.

He gently gathered me up

and lifted me on his donkey like I was precious cargo.

Now I'm ready for departure.

At the inn where he led me,

he made me comfortable for the night.

In the morning time,

he gave the innkeeper 2 silver coins

kindly stating, *Take excellent care of this man, I'll pay all expenses concurred*

*and any additional ones upon my return.*

A sacrificial deed

a selfless act

unheralded saint,

you Good Samaritan

willing to go beyond

your normal borders & comfort zone.

Don't you Know?

There's a difference between religion and a relationship with Me.

One is about ritualism, cultish like practices

but the latter is God-given and true

about losing one's life not driven by selfish gain

but spurred by giving and truly living abundantly.

For the religious man or woman

a hand is stretched out not clammed shut in a time of need

a blessing not a burden

a gift of the rarest breed

a sharing, a caring with no sparing.

The whole human race

is ineffective apart from You.

You think you have an impeccable character,

well I got some news for you,

you need to be rescued from the consequences

of secularized wisdom & theological error

you've embraced thus far

as your own personal doctrine of fraud,

you fashioned through vain pretensions.

You need Me to grant you a heart of mercy

to extend hospitality

instead of contempt for the misfortunes of others

and a willingness to step in and be a blessing

not a pompous fool believing this can't be my fate

but for the grace of God.

I was rescued by someone not bound

by a human timetable but their Savior their Creator God.

In case you did not know you were created from "one blood." Acts 17:26

Therefore, all people are equal, no one more superior.

We are all descendants from our first parents Adam & Eve.

So no race is inferior or superior to another.

Let's value what God made by cherishing His creation.

Mere words not backed by a godly life are useless babble better left unsaid.

You need mature righteousness combined with faith, peace, love & other God-given qualities.

Keep to My standards

maintain an exemplary track record

based upon My approval & divine appointments not man's .

This is a moral history lesson of self's need to reach out

rather than cater to its whims.

*Inspiration*: This spoken word poem was inspired by "The Good Samaritan" Parable found in (Luke 10:30-37 KJV).

# FROM SCARLET WOMAN TO SCARLET CORD OF DELIVERANCE

Sold to the highest bidder,
sold to gratify the lust of many men.
Stripped of my dignity by their godless deeds for gratification
joining our flesh in unions not sanctioned by God
turning what was meant to be spiritual into a filthy disgraceful bond.
You wallow in indecency.

Your dalliances leave you feeling empty, drained, and broken
longing for more
feeling ashamed
discarded time and time again
picked up by exploiters
paraded before men.
Exposed to the world as a whore
your desecrated temple
made you feel
worthless
shattered and
a useless pawn.
You did not know
that sexual promiscuity reaps consequences
not usually foreseen by its clueless victims.

Sanctimonious individuals have labeled me,
a scarlet woman
Now, I'm shunned by bigots
guided by man-rules & laws
from those who rely on an outward adherence to those laws
but offer no genuine humility and remorse
what they do is for appearance purposes only
bemoaning and espousing views
they utter to appear religiously pious
but they come off as holier than thou
and ignorant of being the recipient of
Christ's greatest gift of all.

You are a stumbling block to the blind.
You chose to judge
not love thy neighbor
in hate,
not love you rebuke.
Your actions decree the foolish treatment
you render upon thy neighbor's head
is your declaration of self-love.
Polluted sanctuary
your testimony is one of broken fellowship between you and Me.
You are arrogant and ignorant of Me.

Oblivious to the living Word
so focused on the written words alone.
Religion and legalism have stripped you of any true faith and what I stand for
you are your own version of a prostitute of hypocrisy.
You observe religion but missed the point of faith in Jesus Christ.
It's easier to be a spectator in your religious life
than to touch people as a life messenger for Christ.

Sadducees, Pharisees, and other judgmental fools
go beyond words
to living radically and authentically for Me.

*Scarlet*, you are by no means a coward
but a woman of bravery.
In rescuing, your enemies without abandonment from fear,
you turned disciple for your family
becoming a part of the lineage of Christ for your loving sacrifice.
You had a defining moment when you chose to rescue your sworn enemies.
This was your turning point
from spectator to participant,
harlot to bride of Christ,
Jericho's own betrayer to Abba's own child.

When I (*Scarlet)* personally encountered Jesus,
I was astonished and shocked
by this daring man and Savior.
He revolutionized my life.
The stories I heard about Him
blur at the Living Word of His presence
He was more irresistible than any other man I had ever known.
I can't live without you and don't even want to live without you.
I was full of skepticism before meeting you,

now I know for myself
you are truly the Messiah.
My up close, and personal view of you has changed my life forever.
I was thirsty and I didn't even know
You were the One to quench my thirst,
till you sent the two spies on that day forever etched on my heart.
You transformed my mind, my heart, my soul, my life, and my world,
turning it upside down to right side up.
You pursued me relentlessly.

Jesus offered His reckless love
with arms wide open in grace.
Jesus' story is the story of love, mercy, and forgiveness.
Jesus you embody the promise of God
who would go to extreme lengths to win back the lost.
Jesus you refused to ignore me
like many others who only accused
and never tried to rescue me from sin.

I (*Scarlet*) stepped out on my journey of faith
trusting in You completely.
My adventure
radically changed the course of my life.
You restored my soul and my heart.
You fought for me,
now I'm ready to stand for you.

I (Scarlet) was told to drape a scarlet cord outside the window of my home in Jericho.
This request seemed a bit bizarre but so did some of the stories I heard about this Christ.
I refuse to let anything to stop me from protecting those I love from annihilation.
The two spies return protected all within the doors of my house.

God's chosen people laid siege to Jericho attacking this so called fortified city.
The destruction of Jericho, my former home,
made the braggers look like fools
for believing it was solidly secure against the army of the Lord.

You (Scarlet) gave up your whoring trade,
one that left you spiritually and physically bankrupt.
The lies that kept you imprisoned to the bed of your iniquities
were loosened by your acceptance of Me as the Lord and Savior of your life.
Now you are a found sheep no longer astray.
You're truly living not indifferent to God,
no longer stumbling and fumbling around in the dark.

You left your barren pursuits of darkness
for a pursuit of the Light.
You replaced my indifference with your love.
Now I can hold my head up high
You no longer cry from shame.
You've been forgiven by grace.
You seriously lived out your faith
helping God's people escape
by defying your own race.
God removed your stigma of the disgrace you bore You are delivered, praise God.

**Inspiration**: This spoken word was inspired by the Story of Rahab, the Scarlet Woman found in (Joshua 2 KJV).

# V. MOMENTS OF LOVE, MERCY, AND GRACE

**"For God so loved the world that He gave his only begotten son that whosever believeth in him shall have eternal life." John 3:16 KJV**

Oftentimes we take our moments of love, mercy, and grace for granted. Are you guilty of taking love, mercy, or grace for granted? Right now, if you have been guilty of taking love, mercy and grace for granted, you need to pause and give thanks for these three amazing gifts from God.

I'm reminded of these three gifts every time I read or hear John 3:16, "For God so loved the world that He gave his only begotten son that whosever believeth in him shall have eternal life." (John 3:16 KJV) This scripture epitomizes love, mercy, and grace. Any one that really takes the time to read, analyze, and meditate on these powerful words will notice that in God the Father sending His only begotten Son that was the perfect demonstration of His love for "whosoever" believes. The word "whosoever" represents anyone who chooses to believe in Him.

Mercy is unmerited favor. How many times have you received this precious gift of mercy? The Bible states, that while we were in sin Christ died for us. He did not wait till we had everything together to present this wonderful gift and opportunity.

Years ago, a pastor shared a great acronym for the word grace that has never departed from my memory. Grace is **G**od's **R**iches **A**vailable at **C**hrist **E**xpense.

John 3:16 KJV speaks of the price that Jesus Christ paid when he gave his son as a sacrifice for our sins and all of mankind's.

Those individuals who turn to the Lord get to experience the gift of grace. God's grace did not die on the cross. Our Heavenly Father is waiting with arms open wide for us to have a change of heart and turn from whatever has caused a separation. He no longer wants you to wander around in the darkness since He has provided His light to lead the way.

There was a time when quite a few disciples turned from the Lord and refused to follow Jesus. Jesus posed this question to His inner circle, the twelve, "You don't want to leave too, do you? Simon Peter answered Him, "Lord, to whom shall we go? You have the words to eternal life." (John 6:66-68 NKJV) Are you going to be like Simon Peter?

When you are tempted to move away from the Lord, remember He has the words to eternal life. God is never the one to move. If we feel like He's distant it's because we moved away from Him. Each day you are given, appreciate the moments we have of love, mercy, and grace.

There's always a chance for us to give out what God has given us. He does not provide us with grace so we can hoard it. God desires us to extend grace to those we encounter in our spiritual journey. Also, we are to impart love and mercy along with grace.

My prayer for you is that your heart will be in the right place to show love, mercy, and grace as you advance forward for God.

# DESTINY ACROSTIC POEM

**Determined Dream**- Birthed by God in my spirit connecting my talents and gifts from above. I'm living my life with a determined purpose of: teaching, singing, writing, preaching, speaking, leading, directing, and producing- spurred on by your every command. My goal is to make my Abba's name glorious and win souls for His kingdom. The sword of the spirit instructs my every move. Lord, You make me marvel at the exploits I do, for You.

**Empowerment**- Knowing God is to experience an anointing, an equipping, and an empowerment to succeed in what you have been called to do. Anointed one, you have been called out, "For such a time as this," to fulfill the purpose and plan I gifted and assigned for only you to do. My character should be evident to all who encounter you from near and from afar off. You have been given all you need for the task ahead of you. You have been called to stand up for what's right and not back down. Christian leader you are to exhibit spiritual backbone not flimsy flexibility that caters to fleshy endeavors that remove spiritual vitality. You have been anointed and empowered for change so be the change agent the world needs to see.

**Sanctioned by God**-My destiny is God-given, therefore, not self-driven. What God values, I value so that's what I vow to do with my life. Lord, I seek Your approval not man's for their approval is fleeting as you know from your own personal journey, for one moment they shouted "Hosanna" and a few days later they shouted out "Crucify Him!" However, your approval remains the same for an eternity. I strive to do only what is sanctioned by my God.

**Transformation**-Since my encounter with my Savior and King my life has not been the same. He transformed my soul, heart, mind, body and spirit. Now that I have Him as the Lord of my life, I live a transformed life. The things I used to do, I don't do any more since I've been blood washed and redeemed by the blood of the Lamb.

**Impossible made Possible by God**-My God specializes in impossible situations that baffle man. Just put Him to the test and see what He will do for you and your plenteous problems or needs.

**Not lost but found**-I use to be lost and did not even know, once you found me, I discovered my worth, my purpose and the reason of my birth. My lost status is a thing of the past since I've been found. Your discovery of me has paved my destiny for sure, now I know I'm on my way to heaven no longer bound in sin and headed for hell's flames. You called me out of my sideline role as spectator to the frontlines as a participant on active duty in the Lord's service.

**<u>Yielded-to Christ</u>**. I don't go my own way for I'm led by God. I follow His way, for all other roads will lead me astray. Where He says I'll go. What He says I'll do. Where He leads me I will follow. I will take the limits off Him that have in turn placed shackles on me for far too long. For as a yielded vessel, I know that obedience is always the best policy at all times. Lord, I embrace the divine destiny you have for me, not my will but thy will be done.

# THE ONLY NAME

I was stranded without hope until you came and rescued me
from the sinful state I did not even know I was born into.
I was headed fast down the broad path of sin,
shame, and deprivation before I even knew your name.

Jesus, the Messiah some call you
but others mockingly say Your name or use it as a curse.
But Jesus is the only name
that has the power to save lost souls and make you whole.

I have discovered a life without Jesus
is a life without the grace of God, a hard life for anyone to navigate.
Let Him touch you with His nail-scarred hands
and leave you with a transformed heart so you can begin your new life with Him.

Your emergence from darkness into His marvelous light causes all flight of sin.
His blood grants you a new soul and new heart
and a grand new beginning.

# LOVE

Your love enfolds my heart,
wrapping me in an
oasis of love ever so tight.

I don't ever want to let go
of my blanket of Heavenly bliss.

The magnitude of your love
far surpasses infinity and beyond.

You are more than I
dared to dream or imagine.

You are all I ever wanted and more
rolled up in an all
encompassing package.

# LOVE ACROSTIC POEM

**L** is for a **_love_** so amazingly unconditional that surpasses all human understanding.

**O** is for the **One** and **Only** true love that remains when all else fails. This love endures through thick and thin, good and bad, happy and sad times.

**V** is for the **victoriously** triumphant way God's son, Jesus Christ conquered sin and death when He died at Calvary and rose again on the third day.

**E** is for the gift of **eternal life** believers receive when they accept Him into their heart, soul, and life forever.

# EVERYTHING

SING

*There's no way.*
*No way, no way,*
*I'm living without you.*
*I'm not living without you.*
*I just want to be free.*

I can live without
a man a child children money fortune or fame
How could I ever think
I could live without
You.

You are
my heart
my life
my love
my joy
the depth of my existence
here on earth and in heaven.

Without you,
there's no me.

SING first verse of my song, *My Everything*

*You're my everything*
*The reason why I sing*
*You're my everything*
*The reason why I live*
*You're my everything*
*The reason why I breathe*
*Oh, Mighty God*
*It's because of you*

I can't even begin to breathe
without You
You created me
from out of the dust.

You breathed life into me
When I was just a fragment of your imagination.

Your spirit
filled me
and caused me to soar
high above adversity of my birth
and my presence here on earth
giving me the air
to breathe
to move
and have my being in You.

You're my source of strength
and my constant supply.

Lord,
there's nothing I can't do with You
so I wouldn't care to try to.

You are
MY EVERYTHING.

# I DON'T KNOW WHY

*I don't know why* people reject Jesus Christ but willingly welcome jerks into their hearts, lives, and beds.

*I don't know why* some parents reprimand their children for the very thing they do on a daily basis, it's like they say do what I say, not what I do.

*I don't know why students thank their teachers for their A+ but want to blame and curse out their teacher when they earn an F.*

*I don't know why* God knowingly sent His only son, Jesus Christ to die on the cross for you, all mankind, and me while we were yet in sin. I don't know of anyone that would knowingly sacrifice their own child even though rejection was forthcoming from even their own race.

I don't know the answer to all my whys, but I'm ever grateful for what my Lord and Savior Jesus Christ did so I can obtain eternal life.

# BEST OF ME

Lord, you are the best of me,
you know all of me,
all my idiosyncrasies,
my life in living color with all its sinful drama.

While I was still a sinner,
you died on the cross for me
and all of mankind.

What vast love you bestowed.
Your love is
indescribable
incomprehensible,
and irresistible.

You did not first say I must be cleansed of my sinful acts, before I could be in your presence,
get some degrees under your belt before I could speak to you, be able to expound on the
Bible from Genesis to Revelation,
or wear a suit and tie or a dress before I could go into your presence.

If there were a list of special requirements,
we all would be rejected for these reasons or another.

Jesus, I'm glad your invitation is for all who believe in your Son.
You say to come just as you are but that doesn't mean to expect to stay the same.

You are the definite choice,
I'll make no matter the cost.
I choose to follow you wholely and live for you solely.
The definite actions statement-steps
are my words, actions, attitudes
as a demonstration of my heartfelt love,
devotion and faithfulness to you.

# AUDACITY OF FORGIVENESS

**Forgiveness' Conception Act I**
It's obvious to me,
but not you
that you need a lesson in the anatomy of forgiveness.

Clothed in humility
I came as a babe
borne of virgin birth.
Mother Mary was the conduit
to bring forth my immaculate conception
that still baffles the minds
of biblical scholars and many others alike;
who try to probe this great miracle with a microscopic vision
failing to see the truth which is closer than their vision.
It all began, when I died for you over 2,000 years ago.
Beaten,
broken,
bruised,
and battered for you.
A crown of thorns pierced my head.
I carried the mechanism,
the device meant for my fatal demise.
The load I carried
represented
all the guilt,
the shame,
the pain,
the hurt,
the sin you came
into this world possessing as a seemingly innocent babe.
I bore it all for you
and I would do it,
again,
again,
and again
if it were only you to be saved,
redeemed,
& set free.
Forgiveness' door was opened wide
for you,

for me
through the price paid at the cross at Calvary
& the resurrection of Me, your Lord,
& Savior.
Once you repent of sin
you need forgiveness
so you can set out on a new course,
a new direction,
a newness that leads to eternal life through Me.
*The audacity of my forgiveness*,
came from my fulfillment of my Father's will
to reconcile mankind and spare them a damned eternity in hell.
Do you have the audacity to forgive?
Or are you withholding it based upon
your own version of righteous indignation
of your right to my wrong
believing that withholding your forgiveness
is not crucial to receiving and imparting true forgiveness not true religion.
Your forgiveness is a fallacy.
It's not a so called self-proclaimed "I forgive you" one minute
and in the next breath you are airing out the dirty laundry
of a falsified brand of forgiveness,
a counterfeit instead of a genuine pardon and impartation.
I'm not distant and far
like many try to portray me
or wrongfully think I am,
because they judge me on the basis
of their ill-treatment they've come to expect
or they willingly dish out themselves
from their cynical worldwide secular view point
not a spiritual awareness
but a spiritual melt-down
convoluted by confusion.

Truth be told,
being a "Christian" does not exempt you
and mean you are walking in forgiveness.
The Bible States, "Forgive and ye shall be forgiven."
Saying you offer forgiveness does not mean you truly grant it
or can truly receive it from the One who bestows it.
The question still remains, can you accept forgiveness
is for you
not the one you feel wronged you?
Forgiveness is to the benefit of your growth and spiritual maturity.
You can play the victim card
for only so long before you become stagnant to your own growth

or choose to be the triumphant victor
in this too long denied forgiveness obstacle rollercoaster course,
because your waiting on someone else
to take the role intended for you as the for*giver.
First and foremost, you have to ask God to forgive.
Admit
believe
confess
repent
& turn away
in order to activate your faith
and place your trust in God,
not you,
nor man.


**Tear Down the Jericho Wall of Forgiveness Act II**
Have you thought of the implications of your words & actions?
Which loudly resound your sharp rejection towards forgiving your transgressor.
Or are you just slinging insults & accusations
to hide behind your protective shield.
God's forgiveness, mercy, and love are not conditional.
Judgmental behavior has clouded
your capacity to think and make rational decisions
not darkened with misconceptions tainted by religion,
or philosophical babble
Your incapacity to forgive or willingness to forgive
has built up this wall that needs to be torn down
Forgiveness should never have to be earned, based on conditions
but given out of love for your Lord.
Have you accepted God's forgiveness?
Or do you throw it away like its insignificant?
Maybe you think you have to earn it?
***Don't you know???***
You are a daughter, a son,
redeemed by the blood of Lamb.
You're already divinely accepted by Me, your Creator, Elohim
and clothed in My righteousness.
**Everything I have is yours.**
Don't relate to Him as you do to humanity
I was much more than a man.
I long to be your Savior, your Lord, and King of your life
Don't put Me in a box that you fashion with your lies.
Am I visible in and through your life
Or do you magnify yourself
your circumstances,
your broken,
& wayward expectations?

**Prodigal Daughter or Son Act III**
Don't become like a prodigal daughter or son,
a person who relinquishes the best thing they could ever have
because they foolishly think they can acquire something better.
This twisted thinking will get something different for sure,
a close-up view of sin's tutelage of you,
that was not meant for your view.
You were not meant to perpetuate sin.
Return to your First Love, Me
if you ever left Me
I AM waiting with outstretched arms
looking from a far off
from where you departed from the right destination to where you ended up lost
left in your wilderness of all kinds of hurt
that you brought on by your own disobedient behavior.
Far, far, away in a distant land, a place opposite your right destination.
Don't remain lost but be found again.
Having what the world offers will leave you feeling void.
Many of you,
are blaming God,
others,
your circumstances,
and allowing your anger,
and bitterness poison & corrode your spirit and destroy your life's blood worth.
Why do you refuse to talk to anybody and forgive anybody?
You blame everyone and everything,
including Me.
This behavior will lock you out of your divine destiny and rob you of greater blessings.
Return back to Me,

My child,
I AM
just a prayer away.

***Don't you Know?***
I rejoice over one sinners rescued life.
**Everything I have is yours.**
Why settle for slabs of life's piggish slop
because you settle for a whole lot of crap
when you can have a feast not famine,
an eternity in heaven
instead of an eternity in hell.
Turn your self-centeredness to a God-centered existence.

I love you
in spite of your own flaws & sin.

Just because you may go to church does not mean you are the church or even like Me,
meaning you truly know Me not about Me
and experience all I have for you.
My plans
My love
My salvation
My forgiveness
My mercy & My grace
& My awesome plans for your life
Be restored in right fellowship with Me.

**Foundation of Christianity Act IV**
Forgiveness is the foundation of Christianity.
You are told to forgive because I first forgave you.
Let not the "root" of bitterness defile you,
causing your fall from My grace ruining your godly character,
don't get,
an eye for an eye revenge.
Stop allowing what's behind you,
stuff that belongs in the past to keep you stagnant and poor in spirit.
I urge you "to press on toward the mark of the prize
of the high calling of God in Jesus Christ."
I can erase negative & sinful memories & thoughts
that can prevent and harm your walk with Me.
Don't let the good of success be a substitute for truly walking with Me.
Forgiveness is for your sake not the sake of others.
Forgive like I first forgave you.
Only I can transform your heart to forgive where forgiveness is absent,
Especially in moments when you hold onto a grudge,
harboring vengeance or want to retaliate.

**Benefits of Forgiveness Act V**
Your forgiveness grants you intimacy with Me.
This is a picture of you with no hidden hatred of sin.
You can know and draw close to Me with no hindrance.
***The act of forgiving*** someone means you bestow My grace.
Your forgiveness means the offense will no longer dominate your life.
Forgiveness is a free gift.
The offense no longer binds me to you,
or you to me.
I forgive for my own sake, not yours
I forgive for freedom
an intimate relationship with You, spiritual health,
mental health, physical health, psychological health, victory,
and productivity.
My failure to forgive is evidence that I am still in bondage.

The desire to be free to love Me, serve Me,
& be a holy instrument
greatly used by Me is an illusion if not backed by genuine forgiveness.
Live in forgiveness
not allowing the shadows & realities of guilt to override my blessings.
Your forgiveness grants the answers to prayer, healing,
growth in Me,
is a testimony to the world,
& keeps the bitter spirit of revenge and anger at bay.
As a redeemed child of God, You can approach My throne,
and ask for what you need your access is beyond 24/7.
Our tempter, wants you to believe the opposite of the truth.

**True Self-Reflection Act VI**
Phantom 4giveness is running rampant in & out of the church.
It's catchy so beware,
watch out for it,
it will leave you
thinking you have forgiven someone
but in reality your holding on to the remains,
the residue of the past indiscretions from before,
disguised by your refusal to dig deep
and deal with the real problem
YOU
You're the hindrance
You are your own stumbling block
not the one you feel betrayed your trust,
who so called victimized you
years ago or in a recent scrimmage in your present darkness.

The tell-tale heart
of your internal monologue
recites your past
failures, faults, & sins
which replay
accusations
you perhaps confessed to God
on your last onslaught of self-condemnation.
The key to forgiveness
is to
forgive self
forgive others
so you can
truly progress.

I'll even dare say,
you need to say a prayer
for those who have sinned against you
and ask Me to forgive them
whether they recognize their own need of forgiveness or not.

There's a right way,
there's a wrong way
which one do you prefer?
To go down the straight and narrow road
is never an easy course
though it produces
the greatest dividends & rewards
in regards to an eternity
paved with golden promises of prophecies foretold.
Many in hell
wish they could do it all again,
nevertheless,
once you have reached your final destination
whether in heaven or in hell
you shall remain
there in paradise
or in the torment you forged
with your I'll-do-it-my-way lifestyle mentality choice.

Are you going
to stand up & fight
against your flesh,
your way
that believes the best defense
is a self-righteous attitude & stance.
Will you battle it out & conquer forgiveness once and for all?
Or will a lack of forgiveness teach you a lesson you long denied.

**Inspiration**: I was inspired to write this spoken word poem for a forgiveness exhibition in New York.

# YOU ARE

You are
my heart
life
love
joy
the depth of my existence
here on earth and in heaven.

Without you,
there is no me.

I can't even begin to breathe

You created me
from out of the dust.

You breathed life into me
when I was just a fragment of your imagination.

Your spirit
filled me
and caused me to soar
high above adversity
giving me the air
to breathe
to move
and have my being in You.

You're my source of strength
and my constant supply.

## VI. REMEMBERING YOU/MEMORY OF YOU MOMENTS

**"Why art thou cast down, oh my soul? And why art thou disquieted within me? Hope thou in God: for I shall praise him, who is the health of my countenance, and my God." Psalm 42:11 KJV**

The moment a loved one dies, you can't help but question why God called your loved one home, regardless of whether or not they had been sick for a while, stricken with cancer, some other illness, or they died suddenly. Although at times a physician assigned to the care of your loved one may give an expiration date only our Creator, Elohim knows our end date. You need to realize that death is inevitable. Everyone can be sure of one thing that death will come to us all. The Bible states this about death, "And as it is appointed unto men once to die, but after this the judgment." (Hebrews 9:27 KJV)

The question that you need to think about is where will you spend eternity. If you know beyond a shadow of a doubt that heaven will be your home, you can rest with a blessed assurance that you will be ready when your time comes. There is no need to fear death as long as you know you are a child of the King of Kings and the Lord of Lords and headed for heaven's celestial shore at your demise. Nonetheless, we should be living in such a way as to not just make sure we reach our heavenly home and destination but make sure we go about kingdom business of soul winning so many others may join us.

None of us ever want to have to say goodbye to anyone they have come to cherish and love. This is why, it's important that we "Cherish Each Moment" we are granted by God. It's imperative that we don't take for granted any time we have here on earth. We need to make the most of every opportunity we have, by telling and showing people we love and care about them. If we live without regret, then when a loved one dies we don't have to soberly think about what we could have, should have, or would have said or did instead of what in reality our actions spoke loud and clearly.

Although it so hard to say goodbye to love ones that must depart from this earth, what we really need to do is prepare to live our life to the fullest. The Bible says, "The thief cometh not, but for to steal, and to kill, and to destroy: but I am come that they may have life, and that they might have it more abundantly" (John 10:10 KJV). Our main concern should be to make our moments, seconds, minutes, hours, days, weeks, months, and years count for eternity. We should be living to hear the word from our Lord and Savior Jesus Christ, "Well done, my good and faithful servant …" (Matthew 25:21 NIV)

Have you ever thought about what will be engraved on your epitaph? What do you want your epitaph to say about you? Do you want it to be said that you added life to your years? Did you make the dash between your birth date and death date count or did you squander your life away? I heard it said that the graveyard is the burial ground of an enormous amount of lost dreams, goals, aspiration, good intentions, great potential, ability, talent, for the young and old, rich and poor, and all ethnicities. Death knows no particular stereotype, religion, academic status, or gender. Once it comes you better be ready or you will wish you had been.

# CHERISH EACH MOMENT SONG

**VERSE 1**
Words can't express the depth of my love and devotion to you.
Oh, mama you are a true inspiration for those who knew you well.
Through thick and thin you stood by me,
Oh, how the years have come and gone,
I want to thank you for your love and support
and believing in me.
And now I can see that nothing is im-possi-ble with Jesus on my side.

**VERSE 2**
I honor you now and even in life for all your hard work that you've done.
In every endeavor you showed me Christ's love^.
You freely gave all you had not holding back your best.
From the little you had much came from it
It was not easy raising six kids but did it with God's help^.

**CHORUS**
I'll cherish each moment, I will
Living each day as if it's the end
Loving people not things always choosing to forgive, I will

I'll pass on your legacy of faith and love
Holding high the banner of Jesus Christ
Pointing people to Jesus with every deed

I'll forever cherish each moment

**BRIDGE**
Your death can't steal the legacy of prayer, love, and praise you leave behind.
Your stamp on my heart will never depart

You may have had your battle with cancer but nothing can steal your powerful witness of faith, praise, and prayer. Even in the darkest of moments you refused to complain, you encouraged your loved ones to cling to the one who has power over death

You may have had a battle with cancer but you beat the odds, with God on your side you're always a winner no matter the outcome

So now you're dancing with Jesus you got the shackles off your feet.
No more pain, no more sickness holding you (2x)

**Inspiration**: This song "Cherish Each Moment" is a tribute to my mother, Annette Jackson who died from breast cancer on Wednesday, October 22, 2008. In 2000, my mom found out she had cancer in her left breast. As a result, she had a mastectomy. However, seven years later doctor's' discovered my mom had breast cancer in her shoulders, liver, lungs, and knees. For over a year my mom fought this cancerous battle. Although some would say my mom lost, I say she won the best prize of all, a heavenly crown. Mother Love, Mother Dear, I miss you. You will forever live inside my heart. Until we meet again, see you later!

# EACH DAY

Each day I thank God for the time we shared together, every moment was precious.

I'll always remember you standing up to testify of the goodness of God in your life.

I'll emulate your godly example following your lead, pointing people to Jesus with every deed.

The values you instilled within us by your godly example of a Proverbs 31 Woman (Proverbs 31:10-31 KJV) will never be forgotten.

Thank you for your unselfish sacrifice so we could see Christ.

Your fruit remains behind both biological and spiritual You're a true reflection of our Father's love.

**Inspiration**: I removed these words from the original "Cherish Each Moment "song. I decided to make these words into a poem since I did not want the song to be too long.

# INSTANT REPLAY

I feel cheated. Something
has been stolen. It's not
money; it's time.

Every day I relive my mom's death. I am
constantly reminded that my mom
is no longer here. The world
should stop,
but the sun shines again
and the next day life still continues.

I'm living a nightmare.

Mother has left the earth
and those of us who remain behind
are still trying to figure out
how to live without her presence.

I'm barely breathing;
I'm going through the motions
of trying to gain momentum.

The ground has shifted under my feet.

How can I let go of my mom
when I want to hold on tight?
The progression of time is stepping over my heart. Will I wake up?

**Inspiration**: In 2008, for a creative writing class, I wrote this poem after my mom's death. It was therapeutic for me to write about something that was so devastating to experience. For several months, after the loss of my mom I felt displaced by her absence. This feeling of loss was nothing like when I lost my father almost eighteen years ago. The woman who birthed me into existence was no longer on earth and I had to regain my footing without her. My biggest cheerleader for my dream of writing was my mom. I returned back to school because of her words of encouragement throughout the years. I remember how she would send me newspaper articles of author's interviews and book reviews to spur me to write. She is the reason I include the inspiration component in my book. She constantly advised me to take note of the reason behind writing a particular piece because she said that is a frequently asked question by an interviewer of an author. My mother believed in my dream of writing and I don't regret taking my steps of faith to write as never before. I dare you to dream the impossible dream and do what God instructs you to do so your dreams can become a reality.

# MISSING YOU

Losing someone special is like losing a piece of yourself.
Each new day is a reminder that the one you love is no longer here on earth.
You wonder if your heart will ever mend.
God wants you to know that He is carrying you through this abyss.
As you face each day without your loved one,
you can rest assured that God is comforting and strengthening you.
Cherish the memories of your loved one in your heart
and pass on the legacy they left behind.


Inspiration: I was inspired to write this poem when a friend like family lost a love one.

# NEVER EASY

It's never easy
to say goodbye
to someone you love.
However, the memories
we have of them will forever be engraved upon our hearts

Inspiration: I was inspired to write this when one of my first cousins lost a love one.

# HOMEWARD BOUND

I know it might be tough
but all you have to do is trust.

I have your loved one in My care,
you have nothing to fear.

They will never be forgotten here,
their legacy will continue to burn bright
though time will pass the memories never fade.

You can rest assured that they are in the Master's Hands so don't worry, just scurry to do
the work of the Lord and you will meet them again face to face at Heaven's Pearly Gates.

Inspiration: I was inspired to write this poem when someone close to me lost a love one.

# FAREWELL

I'm letting you go.
I don't hate you
I love you.
I know I can't hold onto you any longer.
I must let you go or this agony will be prolonged without pause,
I can't continue to deny the reality that our relationship is over.
I can't afford to be left waiting
and hoping for something that will not materialize
And probably never will, but I desire.

To say goodbye was not an easy decision to contend with, but the right one.
I had to step up because you leaving me hanging dry was worse.
I want God's will for you and my life above all else, can't you see?
I reached a hard decision.
I wish I could reveal what's in my heart
However, I am not at liberty to state any part of it.

Anyway, it will just prolong the agony and pierce my heart continuously,
So I must go on without you in my life.
I don't want this relationship to end on a bitter note but a sweet one.
The time we shared was brief but special nonetheless.
I don't regret meeting you and calling you friend.
May God mold and shape us both each day into the image of His Son, Jesus Christ.
Adios, go with God.
Embrace Him totally with all your heart, soul, mind, body, and spirit.

**Inspiration**: In 2002, after a romantic breakup I wrote this "Farewell" poem as closure on that particular relationship. Sometimes in our lives we have to say farewell to someone, whether it's a relationship that was romantic or platonic. I said my goodbye with a desire to please God and follow His will for my life.

# *Conclusion*

I pray reading this book of poems, inspirations, and reflections have made you realize you need to maximize your every moment. These poems were meant to encourage you to observe God in every moment of your life.

There will never be a perfect moment or time to do what you have yet to do. You can't afford to become satisfied or comfortable with what you had, have, or will have. Being too comfortable will prevent you from reaching your full potential.

These powerful words from Dr. Seuss sum up what believers need to strive to be, "Why FIT IN when you were born to STAND OUT!"

You were not called out to be comfortable and complacent but resilient and powerful. Many of us are trying so hard to fit into the conformity of the world that we have failed at standing out for God. We have become adjusted to the things of the world and sacrificed a life of promise, purpose and God's presence.

May you enjoy every moment you find yourself in at any given moment of time, whether you fall under the categories within this poetry book or the place you find yourself in bears another name.

Through each moment may you witness the hand of God even in moments where He seems to be absent, distant, or even silent. More likely, if God seems absent, distant or silent you are the one that has grown lax in maintaining right standing and fellowship with Him. You probably strayed away- abandoning Him. If you find yourself in this predicament all you need to do is confess it and repent (turn away from it) and reclaim your rightful place in Him.

God's Road is by no means Easy Street, but it leads to eternal satisfaction. Whereas, Satan's Road is extremely easy, but leads to eternal damnation. Whatever moment you find yourself in, know Your Heavenly Father will always be beckoning you with arms open wide for you to come, *"For God so loved the world, that he gave his only begotten son, that whosoever believeth in him shall not perish, but have eternal life."* (John 3:16) His special invitation is for "whosoever" that believes in Him. This popular scripture passage is the Christian cornerstones verse that invite anyone that desires to receive this free gift of salvation.

May each moment you experience lead you closer to God like never before. Be determined to make your every moment count for Him. If you are willing to take lessons from each moment of time, God will take you farther than you've ever been.

Don't despise any moment because of its challenges or because it doesn't fit into your plan. Remember, oftentimes the most problematic moments yield tremendous blessings.

While you're still in this not so precious moment, remember, you will come out stronger, better, and wiser. Choose to glean the life lessons God has provided in your situation so you will witness triumph not defeat in every moment of your life. Take advantage of these moments so they don't get the best of you.

Treasure the gifts of the moment lest you miss out on the blessings for the moment from God. Spend every possible moment appreciating and cherishing each moment for once they're gone, it's impossible to recapture them again.

May your every moment bring you closer to the One who loves the most, Your Heavenly Father. I'm praying that you will cherish each moment and fulfill all God desires for your life.

*Photo by JDMG Photography Writing Vision*

## *Author Bio*

Mary E. Jackson loves writing poetry. She has performed her original poems and spoken words at various venues. Also, Mary enjoys writing and singing songs on topics ranging from life to death to legacy. When not writing, she enjoys being with family and friends, reading, singing, watching movies, especially shopping for books, clothes, purses, and shoes, traveling, and delivering messages that transform lives.

Mary's voracious love for reading birthed a desire to write life-changing literature that speaks about the power of faith in God. She has a strong desire to inspire, to motivate, and entertain a multicultural diverse group of people by encouraging and challenging them to live a life of purpose.

Mary is the CEO and Founder of the Charles Annette Redeemed Empowerment (CARE) Scholarship Foundation. This organization is created to honor the memory of her parents. This nonprofit provides financial aid to graduating high school seniors that will attend a post secondary institution.

**JOIN THE CARE TEAM**
To Donate with Paypal paypal.me/CharlesAnnette
Website: care4sf.org

A fun fact about Mary is that she wears purple so much that it has become a signature color. The color purple stands for royalty and since she's a part of the kingdom of God, she's a queen through her spiritual birth."

Mary would love to connect with her readers at:

divineinstrumentofgod@hotmail.com

# Acknowledgments

First of all, thank you for taking the time to read Cherish Each Moment Poetry, Spoken Word, Inspirations, and Reflections. After my mom's death I had the idea to write a poetry book that centered around my mom's last poignant words. Although it's been **over** ten years since her death, her final words, "Cherish each moment" still lingers in my ears to this day. As a result, not only did I write this book I wrote a song by the same title to honor her memory.

Right now, I would like to take the time to thank my late mother, Annette Jackson who was my greatest cheerleader in making my dream of being a published author a reality. Your faith in me gave my dream wings and now I'm ready to soar as a writer.

I would like to express my gratitude to all the people that have helped to offer support in writing this book.

iUniverse, thank you for your support in helping me get this book published.

I'd like to thank Willynn Thompson for editing this poetry book.

Also, I would like to thank my Pastor Latoya Moseley, the Co-Pastor of Bread of Life International Worship Center and one of my best friends for writing an amazing and encouraging foreword for this book.

John Gray of J.D.M.G. Photography Writing Vision, thank you for my beautiful book photograph.

Thank you, Demetrio Henfield for your graphic illustrations. Your artistic depictions helped to bring to life the powerful themes for this writing project.

Last and but definitely not least, thank you Heavenly Father for inspiring me to write this book to commemorate cherishing each moment in life.

# *Synopsis*

After losing her mom to cancer, the author realizes she needs to live out her dying mother's poetic and poignant words, "Cherish each moment." These words led to not only the title of her book, but a song tribute, a discovery of making each moment last, and sharing this journey with others.

In this poetry collection, you'll find the rhythms of an unshakeable heart, inspiration that illuminates the soul, encouragement that beckons you to go beyond present circumstances, and comfort that reaches its arms around you and draws you in.

Join me on an unforgettable journey. Step into the pages of time where each moment is a poetic oasis in a desert. Take the time to live as if the present is a gift from God. Don't you think, it's time to "Cherish Each Moment."

CPSIA information can be obtained
at www.ICGtesting.com
Printed in the USA
BVHW022052181021
619265BV00003B/10

9 781532 08